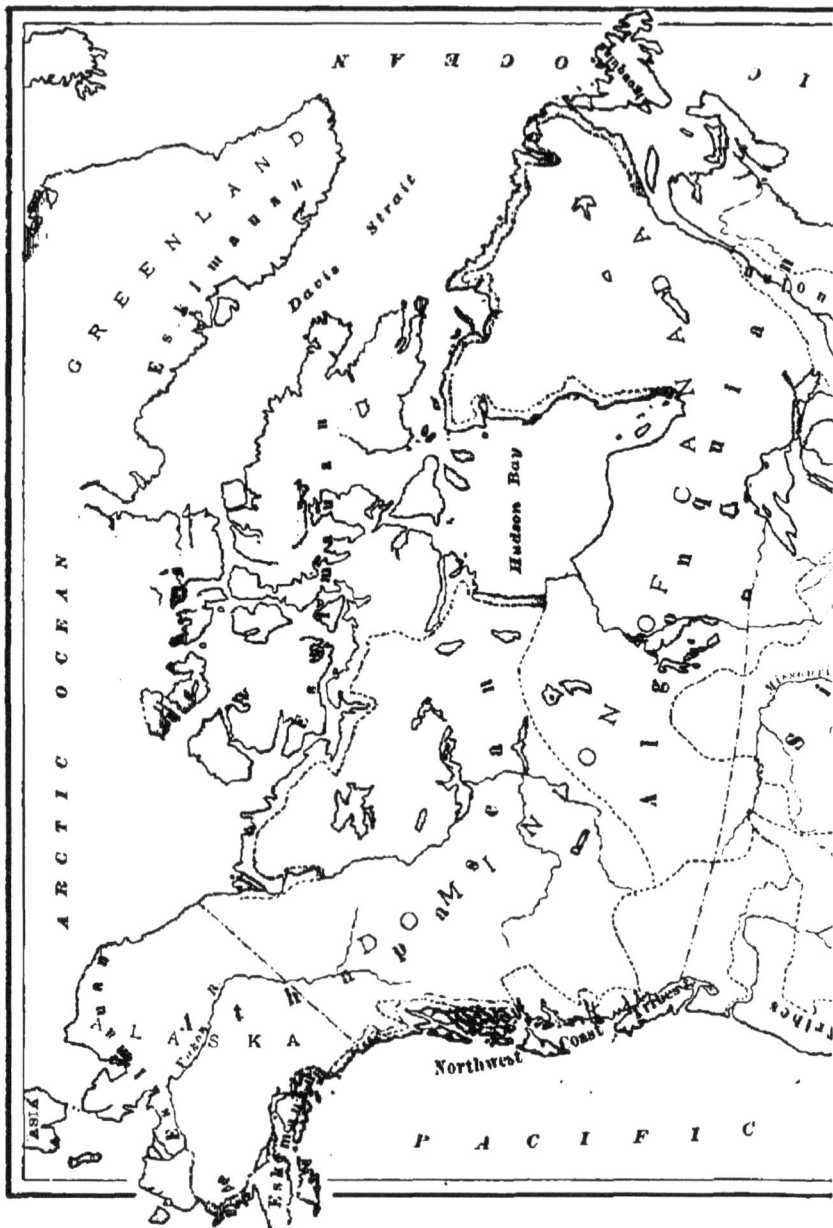

ARCTIC OCEAN

GREENLAND

Esquimaux

Davis Strait

Hudson Bay

ARCTIC OCEAN

ALASKA

ALEUTIAN

Northwest

Coast Tribes

PACIFIC

ASIA

Esquimaux

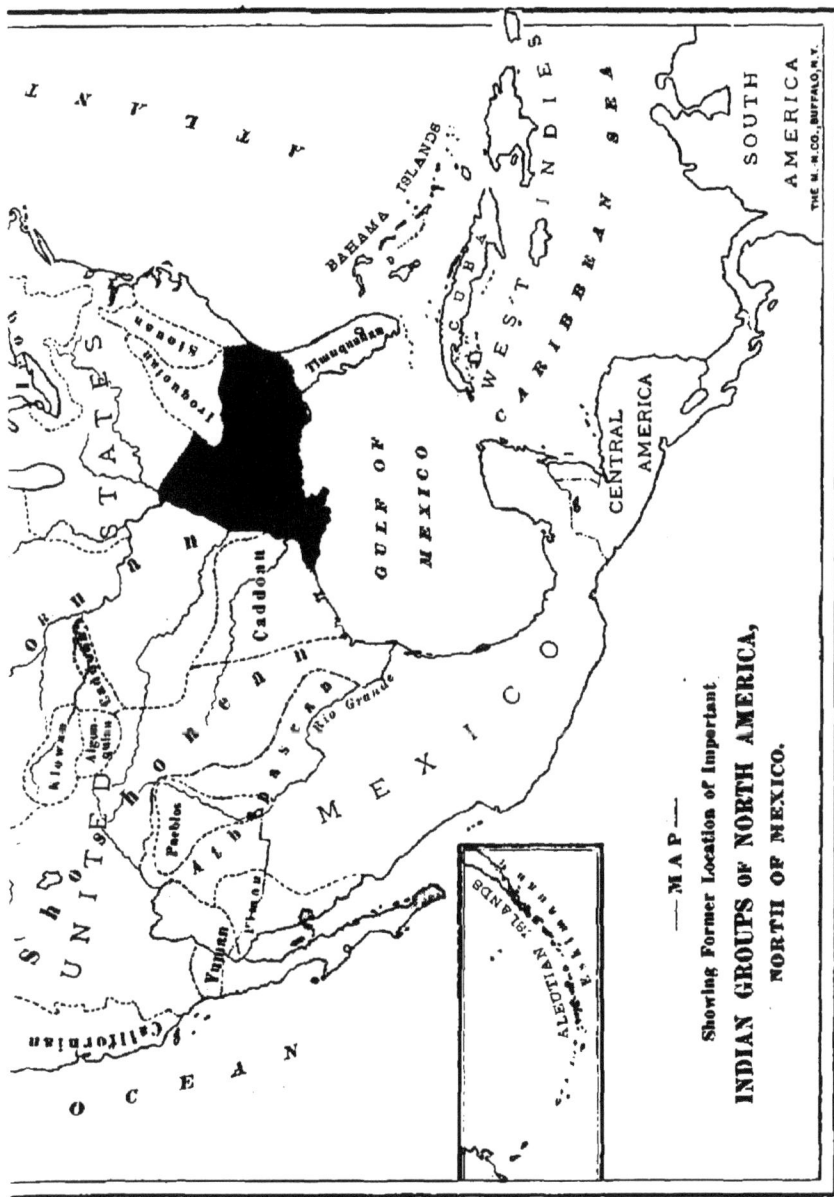

— M A P —

Showing Former Location of Important

INDIAN GROUPS OF NORTH AMERICA,

NORTH OF MEXICO.

ATLANTIC

BAHAMA ISLANDS

WEST INDIES

CUBA

CARIBBEAN SEA

SOUTH AMERICA

THE M. H. CO., BUFFALO, N.Y.

UNITED STATES

Iroquoian

Siouan

Timuquanan

GULF OF MEXICO

CENTRAL AMERICA

Caddoan

Muskhogean

Shoshonean

Algon-
quian

Kiowa

Pueblo

Piman

Athabascan

Rio Grande

Yuman

Californian

UNITED STATES

MEXICO

OCEAN

ALEUTIAN ISLANDS

Eskimauan

Ethno-Geographic Reader, No. 2

AMERICAN INDIANS

BY

FREDERICK STARR

BOSTON, U.S.A.

D. C. HEATH & CO., PUBLISHERS

1899

THIS LITTLE BOOK ABOUT

AMERICAN INDIANS

IS DEDICATED TO

BEDROS TATARIAN

PREFACE.

THIS book about American Indians is intended as a reading book for boys and girls in school. The native inhabitants of America are rapidly dying off or changing. Certainly some knowledge of them, their old location, and their old life ought to be interesting to American children.

Naturally the author has taken material from many sources. He has himself known some thirty different Indian tribes; still he could not possibly secure all the matter herein presented by personal observation. In a reading book for children it is impossible to give reference acknowledgment to those from whom he has drawn. By a series of brief notes attention is called to those to whom he is most indebted: no one is intentionally omitted.

While many of the pictures are new, being drawn from objects or original photographs, some have already appeared elsewhere. In each case, their source is indicated. Special thanks for assistance in illustration are due to the Bureau of American Ethnology and to the Peabody Museum of Ethnology at Cambridge, Mass.

While intended for young people and written with them only in mind, the author will be pleased if the book shall interest some older readers. Should it do so, may it enlarge their sympathy with our native Americans.

CONTENTS.

LIST OF ILLUSTRATIONS.

MAPS.

MANDAN CHIEF IN FULL DRESS. (AFTER CATLIN.)

AMERICAN INDIANS.

I.

SOME GENERAL FACTS ABOUT INDIANS.

WE all know how the native Americans found here by the whites at their first arrival, came to be called *Indians*. Columbus did not realize the greatness of his discovery. He was seeking a route to Asia and supposed that he had found it. Believing that he had really reached the Indies, for which he was looking, it was natural that the people here should be called Indians.

The American Indians are often classed as a single type. They are described as being of a coppery or reddish-brown color. They have abundant, long, straight, black hair, and each hair is found to be almost circular when cut across. They have high cheek-bones, unusually prominent, and wide faces. This description will perhaps fit most 'Indians pretty well, but it would be a great mistake to think that there are no differences between tribes: there are many. There are tribes of tall Indians and tribes of short ones; some that are almost white, and others that are nearly black. There are found among them all shades of brown, some of which are reddish, others yellowish. There are tribes where the eyes appear as oblique or slanting as in the Chinese, and others where they are as straight as among ourselves. Some tribes have heads that are long and narrow; the heads of others are relatively short and wide. A little before the World's Columbian Exposition thousands of Indians of many different tribes were carefully measured. Dr. Boas, on studying the figures, decided that there were at least four different types in the United States.

There are now living many different tribes of Indians. Formerly the number of tribes was still greater. Each tribe has its own language, and several hundred different Indian languages were spoken. These languages sometimes so much resemble each other that they seem to have been derived from one single parent language. Thus, when what is now New York State was first settled, it was largely occupied by five tribes — the Mohawks, Oneidas, Onondagas, Cayugas, Senecas — called "the Five Nations." While they were distinct and each had its own language, these were so much alike that all are believed to have grown from one. When languages are so similar that they may be believed to have come from one parent language, they are said to belong to the same *language family* or *stock*.

The Indians of New England, the lower Hudson region, Pennsylvania, New Jersey, and Virginia, formed many different tribes, but they all spoke languages of one family. These tribes are called Algonkins. Indians speaking languages belonging to one stock are generally related in blood. Besides the area already named, Algonkin tribes occupied New Brunswick, Nova Scotia, a part of Canada, Ohio, Indiana, Illinois, Michigan, and other districts farther west. The Blackfeet, who were Algonkins, lived close to the Rocky Mountains. So you see that one linguistic family may occupy a great area. On the other hand, sometimes a single tribe, small in numbers and occupying only a little space, may have a language entirely peculiar. Such a tribe would stand quite alone and would be considered as unrelated to any other. Its language would have to be considered as a distinct family or stock.

A few years ago Major Powell published a map of America north of Mexico, to show the distribution of the Indian language families at the time of the white settlement of this country. In it he represented the areas of fifty-eight different families or stocks. Some of these families, like the Algonquian and Athapascan, occupied great districts and contained many languages; others, like the Zuñian, took up only a few square miles of space and contained a single tribe. At the front of this book is a little map partly copied from that of Major Powell. The large areas are nearly as he gave them; many smaller areas of his map are omitted, as we shall not speak of them. The

Indians of the Pueblos speak languages of at least four stocks, which Major Powell indicates. We have covered the whole Pueblo district with one color patch. We have grouped the many Californian tribes into one: so, too, with the tribes of the Northwest Coast. There are many widely differing languages spoken in each of these two regions. This map will show you where the Indians of whom we shall speak lived.

Many persons seem to think that the Indian was a perpetual rover, — always hunting, fishing, and making war, — with no settled villages. This is a great mistake: most tribes knew and practiced some agriculture. Most of them had settled villages, wherein they spent much of their time. Sad indeed would it have been for the early settlers of New England, if their Indian neighbors had not had supplies of food stored away — the result of their industry in the fields.

The condition of the woman among Indians is usually described as a sad one. It is true that she was a worker — but so was the man. Each had his or her own work to do, and neither would have thought of doing that of the other; with us, men rarely care to do women's work. The man built the house, fortified the village, hunted, fished, fought, and conducted the religious ceremonials upon which the success and happiness of all depended. The woman worked in the field, gathered wood, tended the fire, cooked, dressed skins, and cared for the children. When they traveled, the woman carried the burdens, of course: the man had to be ready for the attack of ene- mies or for the killing of game in case any should be seen.   Among us hunting, fishing, and dan- cing are sport.   They were not so with the Indians.   When a man had to provide food for a family by his hunting and fishing, it ceased to be amusement and was hard work.   When Indian men danced, it was usually as part of a religious ceremony which was to benefit the whole tribe; it was often wearisome and difficult—not fun. Woman was much of the time doing what *we* consider work; man was often doing what we consider play; there was not, however, really much to choose between them.

The woman was in most tribes the head of the house.   She exerted great influence in public matters of the tribe.   She frequently decided the question of peace and war.   To her the children belonged.   If she were dissatisfied with her hus- band, she would drive him from the house and bid him return to his mother.   If a man were lazy or failed to bring in plenty of game and fish, he was quite sure to be cast off.

While he lived his own life, the Indian was always hospitable.   The stranger who applied for shelter or food was never refused; nor was he expected to pay.   Only after long contact with the white man, who always wanted pay for everything, did this hospitality disappear.   In fact, among some tribes it has not yet entirely gone.   One time, as we neared the pueblo of Santo Domingo, New Mexico, the old governor of the pueblo rode out to meet us and learn who we were and what we wanted. On explaining that we were strangers, who only wished to see the town, we were taken directly to his house, on the town square. His old wife hastened to put before us cakes and coffee. After we had eaten we were given full permission to look around.

We shall consider many things together. Some chapters will be general discussions of Indian life; others will discuss special tribes; others will treat of single incidents in customs or belief. Some of the things mentioned in connection with one particular tribe would be equally true of many others. Thus, the modes of hunting buffalo and conducting war, practiced by one Plains tribe, were much the same among Plains tribes generally. Some of the things in these lessons will seem foolish; others are terrible. But remember that foreigners who study *us* find that *we* have many customs which they think strange and even terrible. The life of the Indians was not, on the whole, either foolish or bad; in many ways it was wise and beautiful and good. But it will soon be gone. In this book we shall try to give a picture of it.

FRANZ BOAS. — Anthropologist. German, living in America. Has made investigations among Eskimo and Indians. Is now connected with the American Museum of Natural History, New York.

JOHN WESLEY POWELL. — Teacher, soldier, explorer, scientist. Conducted the first exploration of the Colorado River Cañon; Director of the U. S. Geological Survey and of the Bureau of American Ethnology. Has written many papers: among them *Indian Linguistic Families of America North of Mexico.*

II.

HOUSES.

THE houses of Indians vary greatly. In some tribes they are large and intended for several families; in others they are small, and occupied

IROQUOIS LONG HOUSE. (AFTER MORGAN.)

by few persons. Some are admirably constructed, like the great Pueblo houses of the southwest, made of stone and adobe mud; others are frail structures of brush and thatch. The material naturally varies with the district.

An interesting house was the "long house" of the Iroquois. From fifty to one hundred or more feet in length and perhaps not more than fifteen in width, it was of a long rectangular form. It

consisted of a light framework of poles tied together, which was covered with long strips of
bark tied or pegged on. There was no window,
but there was a doorway at each end. Blankets
or skins hung at these served as doors. Through
the house from doorway to doorway ran a central
passage: the space
on either side of
this was divided
by partitions of
skins into a series
of stalls, each of
which was occu-
pied by a family.
In the central
passage was a se-
ries of fireplaces
or hearths, each
one of which
served for four
families. A large
house of this kind
might have five or
even more hearths, and would be occupied by
twenty or more families. Indian houses contained but little furniture. Some blankets or
skins served as a bed; there were no tables or
chairs; there were no stoves, as all cooking was
done over the open fire or the fireplace.

ALGONKIN VILLAGE OF POMEIOCK, ON ALBE-
MARLE SOUND, IN 1585. (AFTER JOHN
WYTH: COPIED IN MORGAN.)

The eastern Algonkins built houses like those
of the Iroquois, but usually much smaller. They,

too, were made of a light framework of poles over which were hung sheets or rush matting which could be easily removed and rolled up, for future use in case of removal. There are pictures in old books of some Algonkin villages.

These villages were often inclosed by a line of palisades to keep off enemies. Sometimes the gardens and cornfields were inside this palisading, sometimes outside. The houses in these pictures usually have straight, vertical sides and queer rounded roofs. Sometimes they were arranged along streets, but at others they were placed in a ring around a central open space, where games and celebrations took place.

Many tribes have two kinds of houses, one for summer, the other for winter. The Sacs and Foxes of Iowa, in summer, live in large, rectangular, barn-like structures. These measure perhaps twenty feet by thirty. They are bark-covered and have two doorways and a central passage, somewhat like the Iroquois house. But they are not divided by partitions into sections. On each side, a platform about three feet high and six feet wide runs the full length of the house. Upon this the people sleep, simply spreading out their blankets when they wish to lie down. Each person has his proper place upon the platform, and no one thinks of trespassing upon another. At the back of the platform, against the wall, are boxes, baskets, and bundles containing the property of the different members of the household. As these platforms are rather high, there are little ladders fastened into the earth floor, the tops of which rest against the edge of the platform. These ladders are simply logs of wood, with notches cut into them for footholds.

The winter house is very different. In the summer house there is plenty of room and air;

WINTER HOUSE OF SACS AND FOXES, IOWA. (FROM PHOTOGRAPH.)

in the winter house space is precious. The framework of the winter lodge is made of light poles tied together with narrow strips of bark. It is an oblong, dome-shaped affair about twenty feet long and ten wide. Some are nearly circular and about fifteen feet across. They are hardly six feet high. Over this framework are fastened sheets of matting made of cat-tail rushes. This matting is very light and thin, but a layer or two of it keeps out a great deal of cold. There is but one doorway, usually at the middle of the side. There are no platforms, but beds are made, close to the ground, out of poles and branches. At the center is a fireplace, over which hangs the pot in which food is boiled.

The Mandans used to build good houses almost circular in form. The floor was sunk a foot or more below the surface of the ground. The framework was made of large and strong timbers. The outside walls sloped inward and upward from the ground to a height of about five feet. They were composed of boards. The roof sloped from the top of the wall up to a central point; it was made of poles, covered with willow matting and then with grass. The whole house, wall and roof, was then covered over with a layer of earth a foot and a half thick. When such a house contained a fire sending out smoke, it must have looked like a smooth, regularly sloping little volcano.

In California, where there are so many different sorts of climate and surroundings, the Indian tribes differed much in their house building. Where the climate was raw and foggy, down near the coast, they dug a pit and erected a shelter of redwood poles about it. In the snow belt, the house was conical in form and built of great slabs of bark. In warm low valleys, large round or oblong houses were made of willow poles covered with hay. At Clear Lake there were box-shaped houses; the walls were built of vertical posts, with poles

shed horizontally across them; these were nc
ways placed close together, but so as to leav
any little square holes in the walls; the flat roc
is made of poles covered with thatch.   In th
eat treeless plains of the Sacramento and Sa
aquin they made dome-shaped, earth-covere
uses, the doorway in which was sometimes o
p, sometimes near the ground on the side.   I
e Kern and Tulare valleys, where the weathe

SKIN TENTS. (FROM PHOTOGRAPH.)

hot and almost rainless, the huts are made (
arsh rushes.
Many persons seem to think that the India
ver changes; that he cannot invent or devis
w things.   This is a mistake.   Long ago th
akotas lived in houses much like those of th
cs and Foxes.   At that time they lived in Mil
sota, near the headwaters of the Mississipp
iver.   From the white man they received horse

and by him they were gradually crowded out of their old home. After getting horses they had a much better chance to hunt buffalo, and began to move about much more than before. They then invented the beautiful tent now so widely used among Plains Indians. The framework consists of thirteen poles from fifteen to eighteen feet long. The smaller ends are tied together and then raised and spread out so as to cover a circle on the ground about ten feet across. Over this framework of poles are spread buffalo skins which have been sewed together so as to fit it. The lower end of this skin covering is then pegged down and the sides are laced together with cords, so that everything is neat and tight. There is a doorway below to creep through, over which hangs a flap of skin as a door. The smoke-hole at the top has a sort of collar-like flap, which can be adjusted when the wind changes so as to insure a good draught of air at all times.

This sort of tent is easily put up and taken down. It is also easily transported. The poles are divided into two bunches, and these are fastened by one end to the horse, near his neck — one bunch on either side. The other ends are left to drag upon the ground. The skin covering is tied up into a bundle which may be fastened to the dragging poles. Sometimes dogs, instead of horses, were used to drag the tent poles.

Among many tribes who used these tents, the camp was made in a circle. If the space was too small for one great circle, the tents might be pitched in two or three smaller circles, one within another. These camp circles were not chance arrangements. Each group of persons who were related had its own proper place in the circle. Even the proper place for each tent was fixed. Every woman knew, as soon as the place for a camp was chosen, just where she must erect her tent. She would never think of putting it elsewhere. After the camp circle was complete, the horses would be placed within it for the night to prevent their being lost or stolen.

LEWIS H. MORGAN. — Lawyer. One of America's earliest eminent ethnologists. A special student of society and institutions. Author of important books, among them, *Houses and House-life of the American Aborigines*, and *The League of the Iroquois*.

STEPHEN POWERS. — Author of *The Indians of California*.

III.

DRESS.

IN the eastern states and on the Plains the dress of the Indians was largely composed of tanned and dressed skins such as those of the buffalo and the deer. Most of the Indians were skilled in dressing skins. The hide when fresh from the animal was laid on the ground, stretched as tightly as possible and pegged down all around the edges. As it dried it became still more taut.

A scraper was used to remove the fat and to thin the skin. In old days this scraper was made of a piece of bone cut to proper form, or of a stone chipped to a sharp edge; in later times it was a bone handle, with a blade of iron or steel attached to it. Brains, livers, and fat of animals were used to soften and dress the skin. These materials were mixed together and spread over the stretched skin, which was then rolled up and laid aside. After several days, when the materials had soaked in and somewhat softened the skin, it was opened and washed: it was then rubbed, twisted, and worked over until soft and fully dressed.

The men wore three or four different articles of dress. First was the breech-clout, which consisted of a strip of skin or cloth perhaps a foot wide and several feet long; sometimes its ends were decorated with beadwork or other ornamentation. This cloth was passed between the legs and brought up in front and behind. It was held in place by a band or belt passing around the waist, and the broad decorated ends hung down from this something like aprons. Almost all male Indians on the continent wore the breech-clout.

The men also wore buckskin leggings. These were made in pairs, but were not sewed together. They fitted tightly over the whole length of the leg, and sometimes were held up by a cord at the outer upper corner, which was tied to the waist-string. Leggings were usually fringed with strips of buckskin sewed along the outer side. Sometimes bands of beadwork were tied around the leggings below the knees.

A jacket or shirt made of buckskin and reaching to the knees was generally worn. It was variously decorated. Buckskin strip fringes bordered it; pictures in black or red or other colors were painted upon it; handsome patterns were worked into it with beads or porcupine quills, brightly dyed; tufts of hair or true scalps might be attached to it.

Over all these came the blanket or robe. Nowadays these are got from the whites, and are simple flannel blankets; but in the old times they were made of animal hides. In putting on a blanket, the male Indian usually takes it by two corners, one in each hand, and folds it around him with the upper edge horizontal. Holding it thus a moment with one hand, he catches the sides, a

SKIN JACKET. (FROM ORIGINAL IN PEABODY MUSEUM.)

little way down, with the fingers of the other hand, and thus holds it.

Even where the men have given up the old style of dress the women often retain it. The garments are usually made, however, of cloth instead of buckskin. Thus among the Sacs and Foxes the leggings of the women, which used to be made of buckskin, are now of black broadcloth. They are made very broad or wide, and reach only from the ankles to a little above the knees. They are usually heavily beaded. The woman's skirt, fastened at the waist, falls a little below the knees; it is made of some bright cloth and is generally banded near the bottom with tape or narrow ribbon of a different color from the skirt itself. Her jacket is of some bright cloth and hangs to the waist. Often it is decorated with brooches or fibulæ made of German silver. I once saw a little girl ten years old who was dancing, in a jacket adorned with nearly three hundred of these ornaments placed close together.

All Indians, both men and women, are fond of necklaces made of beads or other material. Men love to wear such ornaments composed of trophies, showing that they have been successful in war or in hunting. They use elk teeth, badger claws, or bear claws for this purpose. One very dreadful necklace in Washington is made chiefly of the dried fingers of human victims. Among the Sacs and Foxes, the older men use a neck-ring that looks like a rope of solid beads. It consists of a central rope made of rags; beads are strung on a thread and this is wrapped around and around the rag ring, until when finished only beads can be seen.

Before the white man came, the Indians used beads made of shell, stone, or bone. Nowadays they are fond of the cheap glass beads which they get from white traders. There are two kinds of beadwork now made. The first is the simpler. It is sewed work. Patterns of different colored beads are worked upon a foundation of cloth. Moccasins, leggings, and jackets are so decorated; sometimes the whole article may be covered with the bright beads. Almost every one has seen tobacco-pouches or baby-frames covered with such work. The other work is far more difficult. It is used in making bands of beads for the arms, legs, and waist. It is true woven work of the same sort as the famous wampum belts, of which we shall speak later. Such bands look like solid beads and present the same patterns on both sides.

The porcupine is an animal that is covered with spines or "quills." These quills were formerly much used in decorating clothing. They were often dyed in bright colors. After being colored they were flattened by pressure and were worked into pretty geometrical designs, color-bands, rosettes, etc., upon blankets, buckskin shirts, leggings, and moccasins. Very little of this work

; been done of late years: beadwork has alm
wded it out of use.

The moccasin is a real Indian invention, anc
irs an Indian name.   It is the most comfoi
foot-wear that could be devised for the Ind
de of life.   It is made of buckskin and clos
; the foot.   Moccasins usually reach only
: ankle, and are tied close with little thongs
ckskin.   They have no heels, and no part

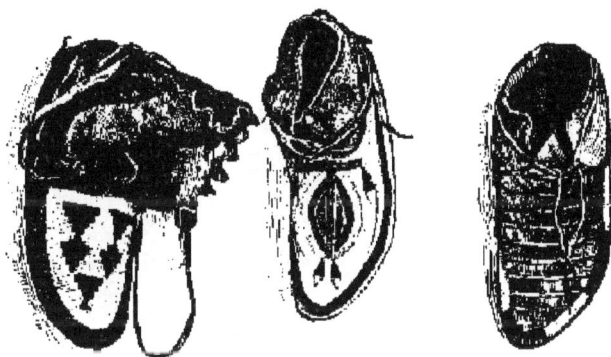

BLACKFOOT   SIOUX   SIOUX
MOCCASIN.   MOCCASIN.   MOCCASIN.
(FROM ORIGINALS IN PEABODY MUSEUM.)

ff or unpleasant to the foot.   The exact shi
the moccasin and its decoration varies with
be.

In some tribes there is much difference betwe
: moccasins of men and those of wom
nong the Sacs and Foxes the woman's moc
i has two side flaps which turn down and nea
ich the ground; these, as well as the part o
: foot, are covered with a mass of beading;
in's moccasin has smaller side flaps, and

only beading upon it is a narrow band running lengthwise along the middle part above the foot.

The women of the Pueblos are not content with simple moccasins, but wrap the leg with strips of buckskin. This wrapping covers the leg from the ankles to the knees and is heavy and thick, as the strips are wound time after time around the leg. At first, this wrapping looks awkward and ugly to a stranger, but he soon becomes accustomed to it.

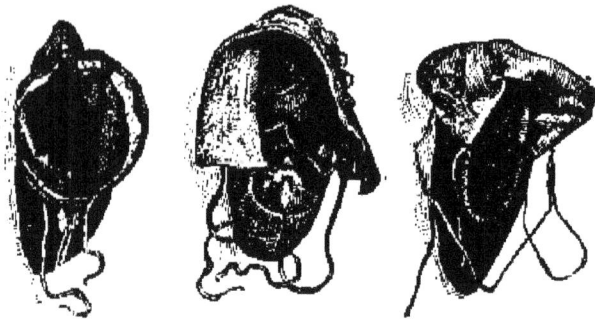

OMAHA   IROQUOIS   KUTCHIN
MOCCASIN.   MOCCASIN.   MOCCASIN.
(FROM ORIGINALS IN PEABODY MUSEUM.)

Not many of the tribes were real weavers. Handsome cotton blankets and kilts were woven by the Moki and other Pueblo Indians. Such are still made by these tribes for their religious ceremonies and dances. Nowadays these tribes have flocks of sheep and know how to weave good woollen blankets. Some of the Pueblos also weave long, handsome belts, in pretty patterns of bright colors. Their rude loom consists of just a few sticks, but it serves its purpose well, and the blankets and belts are firm and close.

The Navajo, who are neighbors of the Pueblos, learned how to weave from them, but are to-day much better weavers than their teachers. Every one knows the Navajo blankets, with their bright colors, pretty designs, and texture so close as to shed water.

Some tribes of British Columbia weave soft capes or cloaks of cedar bark, and in Alaska the Chilkat Indians weave beautiful blankets of mountain-sheep wool and mountain-goat hair. These are a mass of odd, strikingly colored, and crowdedly arranged symbolic devices.

A PUEBLO WOMAN. (FROM MORGAN.)

Among some California Indians the women wore dresses made of grass. They were short skirts or kilts, consisting of a waist-band from which hung a fringe of grass cords. They had nuts and other objects ornamentally inserted into the cords. They reached about to the knees.

IV.

THE BABY AND CHILD.

INDIAN babies are often pretty. Their big
black eyes, brown, soft skin, and their stiff,
strong, black hair form a pleasing combination.
Among many tribes their foreheads are covered
with a fine, downy growth of black hair, and
their eyes appear to slant, like those of the
Chinese. The little fellows hardly ever cry,
and an Indian parent rarely strikes a child,
even when it is naughty, which is not often.

Most Indian babies are kept strapped or laid
on a papoose-board or cradle-board. While these
are widely used, they differ notably among the
tribes. Among the Sacs and Foxes the cradle
consists of a board two feet or two and a half
feet long and about ten inches wide. Near the
lower end is fastened, by means of thongs, a thin
board set edgewise and bent so as to form a
foot-rest and sides. Over the upper end is a
thin strip of board bent to form an arch. This
rises some eight inches above the cradle-board.
Upon the board, below this arch, is a little
cushion or pillow. The baby, wrapped in cloths
or small blankets, his arms often being bound
down to his sides, is laid down upon the cradle-
board, with his head lying on the pillow and
his feet reaching almost to the foot-board. He

is then fastened securely in place by bandages
of cloth decorated with beadwork or by laces
or thongs. There he lies "as snug as a bug
in a rug," ready to be carried on his mother's
back, or to be set up against a wall, or to be
hung up in a tree.

When his mother is busy at work, the little

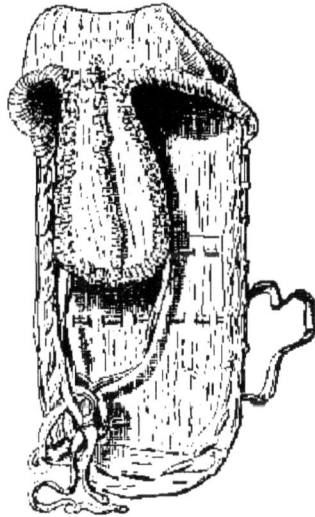

CRADLE OF OREGON INDIANS.   BIRCH-BARK CRADLE FROM YUKON
(AFTER MASON.)   RIVER, ALASKA.

one is unwrapped so as to set his arms and
hands free, and is then laid upon the blankets
and cloths, and left to squirm and amuse himself as best he can.

The mother hangs all sorts of beads and
bright and jingling things to the arch over the
baby's head. When he lies strapped down, the

mother sets all these things to jingling, and
the baby lies and blinks at them in great won-
der.   When his little hands are free to move,
the baby himself tries to strike and handle the
bright and noisy things.

In the far north the baby-board is made of

BLACKFEET CRADLE, MADE OF LAT-   MOKI CRADLE : FRAME OF FINE
    TICE-WORK AND LEATHER.   WICKER.
            (AFTER MASON.)

birch bark and has a protecting hood over the
head; among some tribes of British Columbia,
it is dug out of a single piece of wood in the
form of a trough or canoe; among the Chinooks
it has a head-flattening board hinged on, by
which the baby's head is changed in form; one
baby-board from Oregon was shaped like a great

arrowhead, covered with buckskin, with a sort of
pocket in front in which the little fellow was
laced up; among some tribes in California, the
cradle is made of basket work and is shaped
like a great moccasin; some tribes of the southwest make the cradle of canes or slender sticks

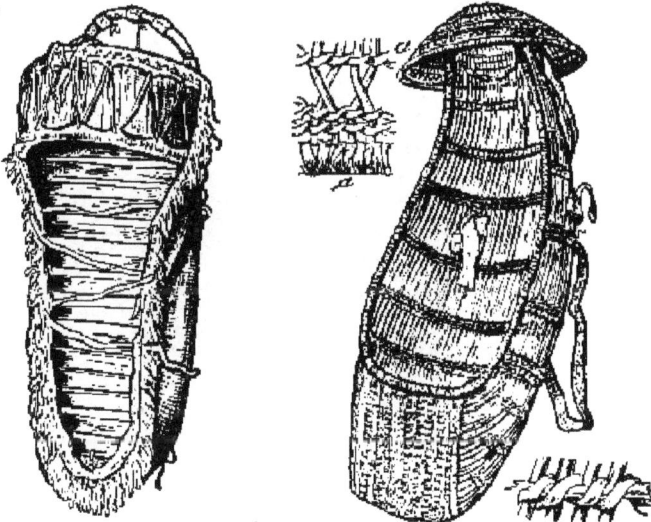

APACHE CRADLE.   HUPA WICKER CRADLE.
(AFTER MASON.)

set side by side and spliced together; among
some Sioux the cradle is covered completely at
the sides with pretty beadwork, and two slats
fixed at the edges project far beyond the upper
end of the cradle.

But the baby is not always kept down on the
cradle-board. Sometimes among the Sacs and
Foxes he is slung in a little hammock, which

s quickly and easily made.   Two cords
stretched side by side from tree to tree

CREE SQUAW AND PAPOOSE. (FROM PHOTOGRAPH.)

blanket is then folded until its width is
more than the length of the baby; its end
hen folded around the cords and made to

lap midway between them. After the cords are up, a half a minute is more than time enough to make a hammock out of a blanket. And a more comfortable little pouch for a baby could not be found.

Among the Pueblos they have a swinging cradle. It consists of a circular or oval ring made of a flexible stick bent and tied together at the ends. Leather thongs are laced back and forth across it so as to make an open netting. The cradle is then hung from the rafters by cords. In it the baby swings.

The baby who is too large for his baby-board is carried around on his mother's or sister's, or even his brother's, back. The little wriggler is laid upon the back, and then the blanket is bound around him to hold him firmly, often leaving only his head in sight, peering out above the blanket. With her baby fastened upon her back in this way the mother works in the fields or walks to town.

Among some tribes, particularly in the southern states and in Mexico, the baby strides the mother's back, and a little leg and foot hang out on either side from the blanket that holds him in place. Among some tribes in California the women use great round baskets tapering to a point below; these are carried by the help of a carrying strap passing around the forehead. During the season of the salmon fishing these baskets are used in carrying fish; at such times baby and fish are thrown into the basket together and carried along.

The Indian boys play many games. When I used to meet Sac and Fox boys in the spring-time, each one used to have with him little sticks made of freshly cut branches of trees. These had the bark peeled off so they would slip better. They were cut square at one end, and bluntly pointed at the other. Each boy had several of these, so marked that he would know his own. When two boys agreed to play, one held one of his sticks, which was perhaps three feet long and less than half an inch thick, between his thumb and second finger, with the forefinger against the squared end and the pointed end forward. He then sent it sliding along on the grass as far as it would go. Then the other boy took his turn, trying of course to send his farther.

The young men have a somewhat similar game, but their sticks are carefully made of hickory and have a blunt-pointed head and a long slender tail or shaft. These will skim a long way over snow when it has a crust upon it.

One gambling game is much played by big boys and young men among the Sacs and Foxes. It is called moccasin. It is a very stupid game, but the Indians are fond of it. Some moccasins are turned upside down, and one player conceals under one of them a small ball or other object. Another tries then to guess where the ball lies.

Many of the Indian tribes had some form of ball game. Sometimes all the young men of a town would take part. The game consisted in driving the ball over a goal. The players on both sides were much in earnest, and the games were very exciting. In the play a racket was used consisting of a stick frame and a netting of

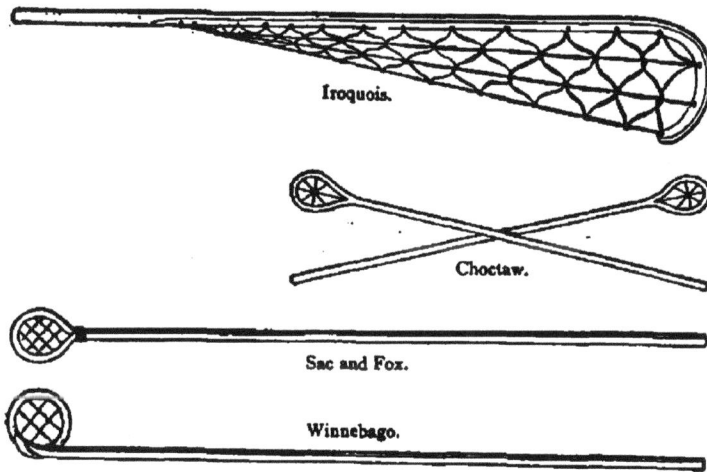

Iroquois.

Choctaw.

Sac and Fox.

Winnebago.

GROUP OF BALL STICKS.

thongs. The shape of this racket or ball stick differed among different tribes. Sometimes one racket was used by one player, sometimes two. Among the Iroquois the game is called by the French name of lacrosse. The young men of one village often played against those of another. They used a curious long racket consisting of a curved stick with netting across the bend. The

Choctaws, Cherokees, and other tribes near them have two rackets for each player.

Catlin tells us that in their games there would sometimes be six to eight hundred or a thousand young men engaged. He says: " I have made it an uniform rule, whilst in the Indian country, to attend every ball-play I could hear of, if I could do it by riding a distance of twenty or thirty miles; and my usual custom has been on such occasions to straddle the back of my horse and look on to the best advantage. In this way I have sat, and oftentimes reclined and almost dropped from my horse's back, with irresistible laughter at the succession of droll tricks and kicks and scuffles which ensue, in the almost superhuman struggles for the ball. Their plays generally commence at about nine o'clock, or near it, in the morning; and I have more than once balanced myself on my pony from that time till nearly sundown, without more than one minute of intermission at a time, before the game has been decided."

But these great games of ball with hundreds of players are quite past, and the sport, where still kept up, grows less and less each year.

OTIS T. MASON. — Ethnologist. In charge of the department of Ethnology in the U. S. National Museum, Washington. Has written some books and many articles. Among the last is *Cradles of the American Aborigines*.

GEORGE CATLIN. — Artist and traveler. See XXII.

V.

STORIES OF INDIANS.

THE Indians everywhere are fond of stories. Some of their stories are about themselves and their own deeds; others recount the past deeds of the tribe; many are about some wise and good man, who lived long ago, and who taught them how they should live and what dances and cere- monies they should perform; some are attempts to explain why things are as they are; others tell of the creation of the world.

Of these many stories some may be told at any time and anywhere, while others are sacred and must only be told to certain persons on particular occasions. Among some tribes the " old stories " must not be told in the summer when the trees are full of green leaves, for the spirits of the leaves can listen; but when winter comes, and snow lies on the ground, and the leaves have fallen, and the trees appear to be dead, then they may tell their stories about the camp-fire in safety. We can give only a few of these stories from three different tribes.

AN IROQUOIS STORY OF THE PLEIADES.

You all know the stars that are called the Pleiades. Sometimes, but wrongly, they are called the Little Dipper. They are a group of seven little stars that look as if they were quite close together.

The Iroquois tell this story about them: There were once seven little Indian boys who were great friends. Every evening they used to come to a little mound to dance and feast. They would first eat their corn and beans, and then one of their number would sit upon the mound and sing, while the others danced around the mound. One time they thought they would have a much grander feast than usual, and each agreed upon what he would bring for it. But their parents would not give them what they wanted, and the little lads met at the mound without their feast. The singer took his place and began his song, while his companions started to dance. As they danced they forgot their sorrows and "their heads and hearts grew lighter," until at last they flew up into the air. Their parents saw them as they rose, and cried out to them to return; but up and up they went until they were changed into the seven stars. Now, one of the Pleiades is dimmer than the rest, and they say that it is the little singer, who is homesick and pale because he wants to return but cannot.

A STORY OF GLOOSKAP.

The Algonkin tribes of Nova Scotia, Canada, and New England had a great many stories about a great hero named Glooskap. They believed he was a great magician and could do wonders. In stories about him it is common to have him strive with other magicians to see which one can do the greatest wonders and over-power the other. Glooskap always comes out ahead in these strange contests.

Usually Glooskap is good to men, but only when they are true and honest. He used to give people who visited him their wish. But if they were bad, their wish would do them far more harm than good.

One of the Glooskap stories tells of how he fought with some giant sorcerers at Saco. There was an old man who had three sons and a daughter. They were all giants and great magicians. They did many wicked things, and killed and ate every one they could get at. It happened that when he was young, Glooskap had lived in this family, but then they were not bad. When he heard of their dreadful ways he made up his mind to go and see if it was all true, and if it were so, to punish them. So he went to the house. The old man had only one eye, and the hair on one half of his head was gray. The first thing Glooskap did was to change himself so that he looked exactly like the old man; no one could tell which was which. And they sat talking together. The sons, hear-ing them, drew near to kill the stranger, but could not tell which was their father, so they said, " He must be a great magician, but we will get the better of him." So the sister giant took a whale's tail, and cooking it, offered it to the stranger. Glooskap took it. Then the eldest brother came in, and seizing the food, said, "This is too good for a beggar like you."

Glooskap said, "What is given to me is mine: I will take it." And he simply *wished* and it returned.

The brothers said, "Indeed he is a great magician, but we will get the better of him."

So when he was through eating, the eldest brother took up the mighty jawbone of a whale, and to show that he was strong bent it a little. But Glooskap took it and snapped it in two be-between his thumb and finger. And the giant brothers said again, "Indeed he is a great magi-cian, but we will get the better of him."

Then they tested him with strong tobacco which no one but great magicians could possibly smoke. Each took a puff and inhaled it and blew the smoke out through his nose to show his strength. But Glooskap took the great pipe and filled it full, and at a single puff burnt all the tobacco to ashes and inhaled all the smoke and puffed it out through his nostrils.

When they were beaten at smoking, the giants proposed a game of ball and went out into the sandy plain by the riverside. And the ball they used was thrown upon the ground. It was really a dreadful skull, that rolled and snapped at Glooskap's heels, and if he had been a common man or a weak magician it would have bitten his foot off. But Glooskap laughed and broke off a tip of a tree branch for *his* ball and set it to rolling. And it turned into a skull ten times more dreadful than the other, and it chased the wicked giants as a lynx chases a rabbit. As they fled Glooskap stamped upon the sand with his foot, and sang a magic song. And the river rose like a mighty flood, and the bad magicians, changed into fishes, floated away in it and caused men no more trouble.

SCAR-FACE: A BLACKFOOT STORY.

There was a man who had a beautiful daughter. Each of the brave and handsome and rich young men had asked her to marry him, but she had always said No, that she did not want a husband. When at last her father and mother asked her why she would not marry some one, she told them the sun had told her he loved her and that she should marry no one without his consent.

Now there was a poor young man in the village, whose name was Scar-face. He was a good-looking young man except for a dreadful scar across his face. He had always been poor, and had no relatives and no friends. One day when all the rich young men had been refused by the beautiful girl, they began to tease poor Scar-face. They said to him: —

"Why don't you ask that girl to marry you? You are so rich and handsome."

Scar-face did not laugh at their unkind joke, but said, " I will go."

He asked the girl, and she liked him because he was good; and she was willing to have him for her husband. So she said: " I belong to the sun. Go to him. If he says so, I will marry you."

Then Scar-face was very sad, for who could know the way to the sun? At last he went to an old woman who was kind of heart. He asked her to make him some moccasins, as he was going on a long journey. So she made him seven pairs and gave him a sack of food, and he started.

Many days he traveled, keeping his food as long as he could by eating berries and roots or some animal that he killed. At last he came to the house of a wolf.

" Where are you going? " asked the wolf.

" I seek the place where the sun lives," said Scar-face.

"I know all the prairies, the valleys, and the mountains, but I don't know the sun's home," said the wolf; " but ask the bear; he may know."

The next night the young man reached the bear's house. " I know not where he stops. I know much country, but I have never seen the lodge. Ask the badger; he is smart," said the bear.

The badger was in his hole and was rather cross at being disturbed. He did not know the sun's house, but said perhaps the wolverine would know. Though Scar-face searched the woods, he could not find the wolverine.

In despair he sat down to rest. He cried to the wolverine to pity him, that his moccasins were worn out and his food gone.

The wolverine appeared. "Ah, I know where he lives; to-morrow you shall see: it is beyond the great water."

The next morning the wolverine put the young man on the trail, and at last he came to a great water. Here his courage failed; he was in despair. There was no way to cross. Just then two swans appeared and asked him about himself.

When he told his story, they took him safely over. "Now," said they, as he stepped ashore, "you are close to the sun's house. Follow that trail."

Scar-face soon saw some beautiful things in the path, — a war-shirt, shield, bow, and arrow. But he did not touch them.

Soon he came upon a handsome young man whose name was Morning Star. He was the child of the sun and the moon. They became great friends.

Together they went to the house of the sun, and there Morning Star's mother was kind to Scar-face because her son told her that Scar-face had not stolen his pretty things. When the sun came home at night, the moon hid Scar-face under some skins, but the sun knew at once that some one was there. So they brought him forth and told him he should always be with Morning Star as his comrade. And one day he saved his friend's life from an attack of long-beaked birds down by the great water.

Then the sun and moon were happy over what he had done and asked what they could do for him. And Scar-face told them his story, and the sun told him he should marry his sweetheart. And he took the scar from his face as a sign to the girl. They gave him many beautiful presents, and the sun taught him many things, and how the medicine lodge should be built and how the dance should be danced, and at last Scar-face parted from them, and went home over the Milky Way, which is a bridge connecting heaven and earth.

And he sat, as is the custom of strangers coming to a town, on the hill outside the village. At last the chief sent young men to invite him to the village, and they did so. When he threw aside his blanket, all were surprised, for they knew him. But he wore rich clothing, he had a beautiful bow and arrow, and his face no longer bore the scar. And when he came into the village, he found the girl, and she knew that he had been to the sun, and she loved him, and they were married.

ERMINNIE A. SMITH. — A highly accomplished woman. Shortly before her death she made a study for the Bureau of American Ethnology upon *Myths of the Iroquois*.

CHARLES GODFREY LELAND. — Poet, prose writer, and traveler. His poems appear under the *nom de plume* of " Hans

Breitmann." His *Algonquin Legends of New England* is important.

GEORGE BIRD GRINNELL.—Writer. His *Pawnee Hero Stories and Folk-Tales* and *Blackfoot Lodge Tales* are charming works. We have drawn upon him for much material, especially here and in XVI. and XX.

VI.

WAR.

ALL Indians were more or less warlike; a few tribes, however, were eminent for their passion for war. Such, among eastern tribes, were the Iroquois; among southwestern tribes, the Apaches; and in Mexico, the Aztecs.

The purpose in Indian warfare was, everywhere, to inflict as much harm upon the enemy, and to receive as little as possible.

The causes of war were numerous — trespassing on tribal territory, stealing ponies, quarrels between individuals.

In their warfare stealthiness and craft were most important. Sometimes a single warrior crept silently to an unsuspecting camp that he might kill defenseless women, or little children, or sleeping warriors, and then as quietly he withdrew with his trophies.

In such approaches, it was necessary to use every help in concealing oneself. Of the Apaches it is said: " He can conceal his swart body amidst the green grass, behind brown shrubs or

INDIAN SPEARS, SHIELD, AND QUIVER OF ARROWS.

gray rocks, with so much address and judgment that any one but the experienced would pass him by without detection at the distance of three or four yards. Sometimes they will envelop themselves in a gray blanket, and by an artistic sprinkling of earth will so resemble a granite bowlder as to be passed within near range without suspicion. At others, they will cover their person with freshly gathered grass, and lying prostrate, appear as a natural portion of the field. Again, they will plant themselves among the yuccas, and so closely imitate their appearance as to pass for one of them."

At another time the Indian warrior would depend upon a sudden dash into the midst of the enemy, whereby he might work destruction and be away before his presence was fairly realized.

Clark tells of an unexpected assault made upon a camp by some white soldiers and Indian scouts. One of these scouts, named Three Bears, rode a horse that became unmanageable, and dashed with his rider into the very midst of the now angry and aroused enemy. Shots flew around him, and his life was in great peril. At that moment his friend, Feather-on-the-head, saw his danger. He dashed in after Three Bears. As he rode, he dodged back and forth, from side to side, in his saddle, to avoid shots. At the very center of the village, Three Bears' horse fell dead. Instantly, Feather-on-the-head, sweeping past, caught up his friend behind him on his own horse, and they were gone like a flash.

A favorite device in war was to draw the enemy into ambush. An attack would be made with a small part of the force. This would seem to make a brave assault, but would then fall back as if beaten. The enemy would press on in pursuit until some bit of woods, some little hollow, or some narrow place beneath a height, was reached. Then suddenly the main body of attack, which had been carefully concealed, would rise to view on every side, and a massacre would ensue.

After the white man brought horses, the war expeditions were usually trips for stealing ponies. These, of course, were never common among eastern tribes; they were frequent among Plains Indians. Some man dreamed that he knew a village of hostile Indians where he could steal horses. If he were a brave and popular man, companions would promptly join him, on his announcing that he was going on an expedition. When the party was formed, the women prepared food, moccasins, and clothing. When ready, the party gathered in the medicine lodge, where they gashed themselves, took a sweat, and had prayers and charms repeated by the medicine man. Then they started. If they were to go far, at first they might travel night and day. As they neared their point of attack, they became more cautious, traveling only at night, and remaining concealed during the daylight. When they found a village or camp with horses, their care was redoubled. Waiting for night, they then approached rapidly but silently.

Each man worked by himself. Horses were quickly loosed and quietly driven away. When at a little distance from the village they gathered together, mounted the stolen animals, and fled. Once started, they pressed on as rapidly as possible.

It was the ambition of every Plains Indian to count *coup*. *Coup* is a French word, meaning a stroke or blow. It was considered an act of great

bravery to go so near to a live enemy as to touch
him with the hand, or to strike him with a short
stick, or a little whip. As soon as an enemy had
been shot and had fallen, three or four often would
rush upon him, anxious to be the first one to
touch him, and thus count *coup*.

There was really great danger in this, for a
fallen enemy need not be badly injured, and may
kill one who closely approaches him. More than
this, when seriously injured and dying, a man in
his last struggles is particularly dangerous. It
was the ambition of every Indian youth to make
coup for the first time, for thereafter he was considered brave, and greatly respected. Old men
never tired of telling of the times they had made
coup, and one who had thus touched dreaded enemies many times was looked upon as a mighty
warrior.

Among certain tribes it was the custom to
show the number of enemies killed by the wearing of war feathers. These were usually feathers
of the eagle, and were cut or marked to show
how many enemies had been slain. Among the
Dakotas a war feather with a round spot of red
upon it indicated one enemy slain; a notch in
the edge showed that the throat of an enemy was
cut; other peculiarities in the cut, trim, or colora-
tion told other stories. Of course, such feathers
were highly prized.

Every one has seen pictures of war bonnets
made of eagle feathers. These consisted of a

crown or band, fitting the head, from which rose
a circle of upright feathers; down the back hung
a long streamer, a band of cloth sometimes reaching the ground, to which other feathers were attached so as to make a great crest. As many as
sixty or seventy feathers might be used in such a
bonnet, and, as one eagle only supplies a dozen,
the bonnet represented the killing of five or six
birds. These bonnets were often really worn in
war, and were believed to protect the wearer from
the missiles of the enemy.

The trophy prized above all others by American Indians was the scalp. Those made in later
days by the Sioux consist of a small disk of
skin from the head, with the attached hair. It
was cut and torn from the head of wounded
or dead enemies. It was carefully cleaned and
stretched on a hoop; this was mounted on a stick
for carrying. The skin was painted red on the
inside, and the hair arranged naturally. If the
dead man was a brave wearing war feathers, these
were mounted on the hoop with the scalp.

It is said that the Sioux anciently took a much
larger piece from the head, as the Pueblos always
did. Among the latter, the whole haired skin,
including the ears, was torn from the head. At
Cochiti might be seen, until lately, ancient scalps
with the ears, and in these there still remained
the green turquoise ornaments.

While enemies were generally slain outright,
such was not always the case. When prisoners,

one of three other fates might await them: they might be adopted by some member of the tribe, in place of a dead brother or son; they might

be made to run the gauntlet as a last and desperate chance of life. This was a severe test of agility, strength, and endurance. A man, given this chance, was obliged to run between two lines of Indians, all more or less armed, who struck at him as he passed. Usually the poor wretch fell, covered with wounds, long before he reached the end of the lines; if he passed through, however, his life was spared. Lastly, prisoners might be tortured to death, and dreadful accounts exist of such tortures among

APACHE AND SIOUX SCALPS.

Iroquois, Algonkin and others. One of the least terrible was as follows: the unfortunate prisoner was bound to the stake, and the men and women picked open the flesh all over the body with knives; splinters of pine were then driven into the wounds and set on fire. The prisoner died in dreadful agony.

VII.

HUNTING AND FISHING.

To the Indian hunting and fishing were serious business.   Upon the man's success depended the comfort and even the life of the household. Game was needed as food.   The Indians had to learn the habits of the different animals so as to be able to capture or kill them.   Boys tried early to learn how to hunt.

Clark tells of an Indian, more than eighty years old, who recalled with great delight the pleasure caused by his first exploit in hunting. "When I was eight years of age," he said, "I killed a goose with a bow and arrow and took it to my father's lodge, leaving the arrow in it. My father asked me if I had killed it, and I said, 'Yes; my arrow is in it.' My father examined the bird, fired off his gun, turned to an old man who was in the lodge, presented the gun to him and said, 'Go and harangue the camp; inform them all what my boy has done.' When I killed my first buffalo I was ten years old. My father was right close, came to me and asked if I killed it. I said I had. He called some old men who were by to come over and look at the buffalo his son had killed, gave one of them a pony, and told him to inform the camp." Such boyish successes were always the occasion of family rejoicing.

To the Indians of the Plains the important game was buffalo; and for buffalo two great hunts were made each year, — a summer and a winter hunt. Sometimes whole villages together went to these hunts. Few cared to stay behind, for fear of attack by hostile Indians. Provisions and valuables which were not needed on the journey were carefully buried, to be dug up again on the return. At times the people of a village went hundreds of miles on these expeditions. Baggage was carried on ponies in charge of the women. At night it took but a few minutes to make camp, and no more was necessary in the morning for breaking camp and getting on the way.

In journeying they went in single file. Scouts constantly kept a lookout for herds. When a herd was sighted, it was approached with the greatest care: everything was done according to fixed rules and under appointed leaders. When ready for the attack, the hunters drawn up in a single row approached as near as possible to the herd and waited for the signal to attack. When it was given, the whole company charged into the herd, and each did his best to kill all he could. All were on horseback, and armed with bows and arrows. They tried to get abreast of the animal and to discharge the weapon to a vital spot. One arrow was enough to kill sometimes, but usually more were necessary. A single success-ful hunter might kill four or five in a half hour.

After the killing a lively time ensued. The

dead animals were skinned, cut up, and carried on ponies into camp. There the skins were pegged out to dry, the meat was cut up into strips or sheets for drying, or made up into pemmican. Every one was busy and happy in the prospect of plenty of food.

Sometimes, however, no herds could be found. Day after day passed without success. The camp was well-nigh discouraged. Then a buffalo dance was held. In this the hunters dressed themselves in the skins and horns of buffalo, and danced to the accompaniment of special music and songs.

In dancing, they imitated the movements of the buffalo, believing that thus they could compel the animals to appear. Hour after hour, even day after day, passed in such dancing until some scout hurrying in reported a herd in sight. Then the dance would abruptly cease, its object being gained.

Of course many ingenious devices were employed in hunting. Antelope were stalked; fur-bearing animals were trapped or snared. Sometimes all the animals in a considerable area were driven into a central space where they were killed, or from which they were driven between lines of stones or brush, to some point where they would fall over a cliff and be killed in the fall. Such drives used to be common in the Pueblo district. To-day deer are rarer there; so are the mountain lion and the bear. Hunts there are more likely

nowadays to be for rabbits than for larger game.
These are caught in nets, but are more frequently
killed by rabbit sticks, which may be knot-ended
clubs or flat, curved throwing sticks, a little like
the boomerangs of Australia.

The great weapon for hunting was the bow and
arrow. Indian bows ranged from frail, weak
things, hardly suitable for a child, to the "strong
bow" of the Sioux and Crows, which would send

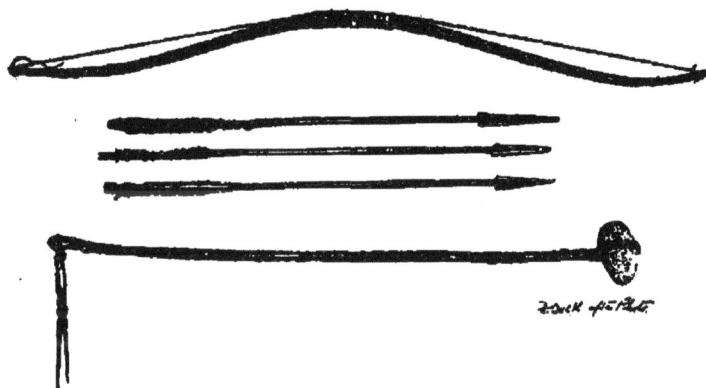

GROUP OF WEAPONS.
(FROM ORIGINALS IN PEABODY MUSEUM, CAMBRIDGE.)

an arrow completely through a buffalo; the most
powerful Colt's revolver — so Clark says — will
not send a ball through the same animal. The
Crows sometimes made beautiful bows of elk
horn; such cost much labor and were highly
valued. Three months' time was spent in making a single one. Arrows required much care
in their making. In some tribes each man
made all his arrows of precisely one length,

different from all others. This was an aid in
recognizing them. Many carried with them a
measure, the exact length of their arrows so as to
settle disputes. This was necessary to determine
who had killed a given animal: the carcass belonged to the man whose arrow was found in it.

Among some eastern tribes, and particularly
in the south, where fine canes grow near streams,
the blow-gun is used. This consists of a piece
of cane perhaps eight or ten feet long, which
is carefully pierced from end to end and then
smoothed inside. Arrows are made from slender
shafts of rather heavy and hard wood. They are
perhaps a foot and a half long and hardly more
than a quarter or an eighth of an inch thick.
They are cut square at one end and pointed at
the other; around the shaft, toward the blunt
end, a wrapping of thistle-down is firmly secured
with thread. This surrounds perhaps three or
four inches of the arrow's length, and has a
diameter such as to neatly fit the bore of the
blow-gun. The arrow is inserted in the tube,
and a sudden puff of breath sends it speeding
on its way. An animal the size of a rabbit or
woodchuck may be killed with this weapon at
an astonishing distance.

Among inland tribes, fishing was usually a matter of secondary importance. Fish pieced out the
food supply rather than formed its bulk. But
along some seacoasts fish is a very important
food. The tribes of the Northwest Coast live

almost entirely upon fish. The salmon is particularly important among them. These tribes
have devised many kinds of lines, hooks, nets,
fish-baskets, traps, and wiers. Everywhere the
commonest mode of securing fish is and was by
spearing.

Once I went out at night with some Indian
boys of Gay Head, Martha's Vineyard, "neeskotting." These boys have a good deal of
Indian blood, but they dress, talk, and act in
most ways just like white boys. I think *neeskotting*, however, is truly Indian. "We rode down

BIRCH-BARK CANOE.

to the shore in an ox-cart, carrying lanterns with
us. Each boy had a pole, at the end of which
was firmly tied a cod-hook. The tide was falling,
and the wind was blowing in toward shore.
Walking along the beach, with lantern held in
one hand so as to see the shallow water's bottom,
and with the pole in the other hand ready for
use, the boys watched for fish. Hake, a foot or
more long, frost fish, lighter colored and more
slender, and eels, are the usual prey. The hake
and eels rarely come into water less than six
inches deep. Frost fish, on the contrary, come

close into shore, and on cold nights crowd out on the very beach. When a fish has been seen, a sudden stroke of the pole and a quick inpull are given to impale the prey, and drag it in to shore. It was an exciting scene. Hither and thither the boys darted, with strokes and landings, with cries of joy at success or despair at failure. Finally, with perhaps fifty hake, twenty frost fish, and one shining eel, the bottom of our cart was covered, and we turned homeward."

In fishing, hunting, and journeying, the wood-

"BULL-BOAT" OR CORACLE.

land Indians needed some sort of water craft. They had a number of different kinds of canoes. The "dug-out," cut from a single tree trunk, is still used in many of our Southern streams; the Cherokees in their lovely North Carolina home have them. Along the Northwest Coast, magnificent war-canoes, capable of carrying fifty or sixty persons, were made from single giant logs; these canoes often had decorative bow and stern pieces carved from separate blocks. The birch-bark canoes were made over light wooden frames with pieces of birch bark neatly fitted, sewed, and gummed, to keep out the water. Almost all the Algonkin tribes and the Iroquois used them upon their lakes and rivers; they were light enough to be carried easily across the portages. A few tribes, the Mandans among others, had the light but awkward " bull-boat," or coracle, nearly circular, consisting of a light framework covered with skin: such were chiefly used in ferrying across rivers.

VIII.

THE CAMP-FIRE.

ONE of the first things after reaching camp was to build the camp-fire. Among Indians the camp-fire not only served for heat and cooking, but for light, and to scare away animal foes and bad spirits. You and I would probably have a hard time making a fire without matches. The Indian had no matches until he got them from the whites. There are two ways in which the Indians made fire. One was by striking two hard pieces of stone — such as chert or pyrites — together, which gave a spark, which was caught on tinder and blown to a flame. Of course white men used to make fire in much the same way — only they had a flint and steel. When whites first came into contact with Indians, they used the flint and steel, and it was not long before the

Indians had secured them from the white traders. Many Indians still use the old-fashioned flint and steel. Some old Sac and Fox men always carry them in their tobacco pouch, and use them for lighting their pipes.

Another Indian method of making fire was by rubbing two pieces of wood together. It is said that this is not difficult, but one needs to know just how, in order to succeed. In the cliff ruins of the southwest two little sticks are often found together. One may be a foot or two long, and the lower end is bluntly pointed, worn smooth, and blackened as if it had been slightly burned. The other stick is of the same thickness, but may be only a few inches long; in it are several coni-cal hollows, which are charred, smooth, and usu-ally broken away at the edge. These two sticks were used by the " cliff-dwellers " for making fire. The second one was laid down flat on the ground; the pointed end of the other was placed in one of the holes in the lower piece, and the stick was whirled between the hands by rubbing these back and forth. While the upright stick was being whirled, it was also pressed down with some little force. By the whirling and pressure fine wood dust was ground out which gathered at the broken edge of the conical cavity. Soon, in the midst of this fine wood dust, there appeared a spark. Some dry, light stuff was at once applied to it, and it was blown into a flame.

Certainly this mode of making fire was hard

on the hands — it must soon have raised blisters. Some tribes had learned how to grind out a spark without this disadvantage. The lower stick was as before. A little bow was taken, and its cord was wrapped about the upright stick and tightened. The two sticks were then put into position, the top of the upright being steadied with a small block held in the left hand; the bow being moved back and forth with the right hand, the upright was caused to whirl easily and rapidly. This was used among many of our tribes.

Although making it themselves, many Indians think the fire made with the bow-drill is sacred, and that it comes from heaven. Among the Aztecs of Mexico there was a curious belief and ceremony. The Aztecs counted their years in groups of fifty-two, just as we count ours by hundreds or centuries. They thought the world would come to an end at the close of one of these fifty-two year periods. Therefore, they were much disturbed when such a time approached. When the end of the cycle really came, all the fires and lights in the houses had been put out; not a spark remained anywhere. When it was night, the people went out along the great causeway to Itztapalapa, at the foot of the Hill of the Star. On the summit of this hill was a small temple. At the proper hour, determined by observing the stars, the priests cast a victim on the altar, tore out his heart as usual, and placed the lower stick of the fire-sticks upon the wound.

The upright stick was adjusted and whirled. For a moment all were in great anxiety. The will of the gods was to be made known. If no spark appeared, the world would at once be destroyed; if there came a spark, the gods had decreed at least one cycle more of existence to the world. And when the spark appeared, how great was the joy of the people! All had carried unlighted torches in their hands, and now these were lighted with the new fire, and with songs of rejoicing the crowd hurried back to the city.

Boys know pretty well how Indians cooked their food. Most of us have roasted potatoes in the hot ashes, and broiled meat or frogs' legs over the open fire. The Indians did much the same. Pieces of meat would be spitted on sharp sticks, and set so as to hang over the fire. Clams, mussels, and other things, were baked among the hot coals or ashes. One time "Old Elsie," a Lipan woman, took a land turtle, which I brought her alive, and thrust it head first into the fire. This not only killed the turtle, but cooked it, and split open the hard shell box so that she could get at the meat inside.

Over the fireplace the Indians usually have a pot or kettle suspended in which various articles may be boiling together. The Indians invented succotash, which is a stew of corn and beans; we have borrowed the thing and the name. At the first meal I ate among the Sacs and Foxes, we all squatted on the ground, outside the house and near the fire, and took a tin of boiled fish off the coals. We picked up bits of the fish with our fingers, and passed the pan around for every one to have a drink of the soup.

All this is easy cooking; but how would you go to work to boil buffalo meat if you had no kettle, pot, nor pan of any kind? A great many Indian tribes knew how. When a buffalo was killed, the hide was carefully removed. A bowl-like hole was scraped out in the ground and lined with the buffalo skin, the clean side up. This made a nice basin. Water was put into this and the pieces of meat laid in. A hot fire was kindled near by, and stones were heated in it, and then dropped into the basin of water and meat. So the food was boiled. A number of tribes cooked meat in this way, but one was called by a name that means "stone-boilers".— Assinaboines.

Meat was often dried. In some districts where the air is clear and dry and the sun hot, the meat is cut into strips or sheets, and dried by hanging it on lines near the house. At other places it was dried and smoked over a fire. Where there was buffalo meat, the Indian women made pemmican, which was *good*. The buffalo meat was first dried as usual. The dried meat was heated through over a low fire, and then beaten with sticks or mauls to shreds. Buffalo tallow was melted and the shredded meat stirred up in it. All was then put into a bag made of buffalo skin and packed as tightly as possible; the bag was

SMOKE SIGNALING. (AFTER MALLERY.)

then fastened up and sewed tight. Sometimes the marrow-fat was also put into this pemmican, and dried berries or choke-cherries. Pemmican kept well a long time, and was such condensed food that a little of it lasted a long time. It was eaten dry or stewed up in water into a sort of soup.

A curious use for fire among some Indians was in giving signals. A place visible from a great distance was selected. Upon it a little fire was built with fuel which gave a dense smoke. Sometimes the signal depended upon the number of fires kindled side by side. Thus when Pima Indians returned from a war-party against Apaches, they gave smoke signals if they had been successful. A single fire was built first; its one smoke column meant success. Then a number of little fires, kindled in a line side by side, indicated the number of scalps taken. Sometimes messages were given by puffs of smoke. When the fire had been kindled, a blanket was so held as to prevent the smoke rising. When a lot of smoke had been imprisoned beneath it, the blanket was suddenly raised so as to let it escape. It was then lowered, held, and raised so as to cause a new puff. These puffs of smoke rose regularly in long, egg-shaped masses, and according to their number the message to be sent varied. Such signaling by smoke puffs was common among Plains tribes.

IX.

SIGN LANGUAGE ON THE PLAINS.

EVERY one talking with another person who speaks a different language will, in his effort to make himself understood, quite surely make some use of signs. Often the signs so used will seem naturally to express the desired idea. Once, a Tonkaway Indian in trying to tell me that all white men were untruthful, put the first two fingers of his right hand, slightly separated, near his mouth and then moved the hand downward and outward, at the same time slightly spreading the fingers. By this he meant to say that white men had two tongues, or were liars. They say one thing and mean another.

While it is natural for all people to use signs to convey meaning, the use of signs will be most frequent where it is a common thing for several people speaking different languages to come into contact. While all American Indians use some gestures, the Plains Indians, who were constantly meeting other tribes, necessarily made much use of them. In fact, a remarkable sign language had grown up among them, whereby Sioux, Crows, Assinaboines, Pani, Arapahoes, Cheyennes, Kiowas, could readily converse upon any subject.

It is not probable that the sign language was invented by any one tribe. Many writers have claimed that it was made by the Kiowas. Rather, it grew up of itself among the tribes because gesturing is natural to peoples everywhere.

Deaf-mutes left to themselves always use signs. These signs are of two kinds. They either picture or copy some idea, thing, or action, or they point out something. It is interesting to find that the gestures made by deaf-mutes and Indians are often the same. So true is this, that deaf-mutes and Indians quite readily understand each other's signs. Parties of Indians in Washington for business are sometimes taken to the Deaf-Mute College to see if the two — Indians and deaf-mutes — can understand each other. While they cannot understand every sign, they easily get at each other's meaning. One time a professor from a deaf-mute school, who knew little of Indians and nothing at all of Indian languages, had no difficulty while traveling through Indian country in understanding and in making himself understood by means of signs.

We will look at a few examples of Indian signs. Try and make them from the description, and see whether you think they are natural or not. The signs for animal names usually describe or picture some peculiarity of the animal.

Badger. — The right hand is held with the back up, fingers extended, touching and pointing to the front, in front and to the right of the body. This shows the height of the animal. Then the first and second fingers are slightly separated (the rest of the hand being closed) and drawn from the nose upward over the top of the head. This shows the striped face. The two hands are then held in front of the body, with fingers curved, the backs up. and drawn as if pawing or scratching. This has reference to the digging of the animal. The complete sign thus gives the size, the most striking mark, and the habit of the animal.

SIGN LANGUAGE ON THE PLAINS.
(AFTER MALLERY.)

Beaver.— Hold out the left hand, with the back up, pointing to the right and front, in front of the body, with the lower part of the arm horizontal; cross the right hand under it so that the back of the *right hand* is *against* the *left palm*. Then leaving the right wrist *all the time against* the *left palm*, briskly move the right hand up and down so it shall *slap* against the left palm. The beaver has a broad, flat tail, with which he strikes mud or water. The sign imitates this action.

Buffalo. — Close the hands except the forefingers; curve these; place the hands then against the sides of the head, near the top and fairly forward. These curved forefingers resemble the horns of the buffalo and so suggest that animal.

Dog. — Place the right hand, with the back up, in front of and a little lower than the left breast: the first and second fingers are extended, separated, and point to the left. The hand is then drawn several inches to the right, horizontally. I am sure you never would guess how this came to mean dog. You remember how the tent poles are dragged by ponies when camp is moved? Well, before the Indians had horses as now, the dogs used to have to drag the poles. This sign represents the dragging of the poles.

Skunk. — The skunk is a little animal, but it has rather a complicated sign. (*a*) The height is indicated as in the case of the badger. (*b*) Raise the right hand, with the back backward, a little to the right of the right shoulder; all the fingers are closed except the forefinger, which is curved; the hand is then moved forward several inches by gentle jerks. This represents the curious way in which the broad, bushy tail is carried and the movement of the animal in walking. (*c*) Raise right hand toward the face, with the two first fingers somewhat separated, to about the chin. Then move it upward until the nose passes between the separated finger tips. This means smell. (*d*) Hold both hands, closed with backs up, in front of the body, the two being at the same height. Move them down and outward, at the same time opening them. This is done rather briskly and vigorously. It means bad. Thus in the sign for skunk we give size, character of tail and movement, and bad smell.

There are of course signs for the various Indian tribes, and some of these are interesting
because they usually present some striking characteristic of the tribe named.

Crow. — Make with the arms the motion of flapping wings.

Arapaho. — The fingers of one hand touch the
breast in different parts to indicate the tattooing of
that part in points.

Arikara, often called "corn-eaters," are represented by imitating the shelling of corn, by holding
the left hand still, the shelling being done with the
right.

Blackfeet. — Pass the flat hand over the outer edge
of the right foot from the heel to beyond the toe, as
if brushing off dust.

Comanche and *Shoshone.* — Imitate with the hand
or forefinger the crawling motion of the snake.

Flathead. — The hand is raised and placed against
the forehead.

We will only give one more example. The
sign for crazy is as follows : —

Slightly contract the fingers of the right hand without closing it; bring it up to and close in front of the
forehead; turn the hand so that the finger tips describe a little circle.

Bad boys sometimes speak of people having
wheels in their head. This Indian sign certainly
seems to show that the Indian idea of craziness is
about the same as the boys'.

Captain Clark wrote a book on the Indian

sign language, in which he described great numbers of these curious signs. Lieutenant Mallery, too, made a great collection of signs and wrote a long paper about them. A third gentleman has tried to make type which shall print the sign language. He made more than eight hundred characters. With these he plans to teach the old Indians to read papers and books printed in the signs. He thinks that the Indian can take such a paper, and making the signs which he sees there pictured, he will understand the meaning of the article.

W. P. CLARK. — Soldier. Author of *Indian Sign Language*, which not only is a convenient dictionary of signs, but contains much general information regarding Indians.

GARRICK MALLERY. — Soldier, ethnologist. Connected with Bureau of Ethnology from its establishment until his death. His most extended papers are: *Sign Language among North American Indians, Pictographs of the North American Indians, Picture Writing of the American Indians.*

LEWIS HADLEY. — Inventor of Indian Sign Language type.

X.

PICTURE WRITING.

THE Indians did not know how to write words by means of letters. There were, however, many things which they wished to remember, and they had found out several ways in which to record these.

Thus among the Sacs and Foxes there is a long legend with songs telling about their great teacher, the good, wise, and kind Wisuka. It is difficult to remember exactly such long narratives, but with objects to remind the reciter of each part, it is not so hard. So the persons who are to repeat the legend have a *micäm*. This is a wooden box, usually kept carefully wrapped up in a piece of buckskin and tied with a leathern thong; in it are a variety of curious objects, each one of which reminds the singer or reciter of one part of the narrative. Thus he is sure not to leave out any part. In the same way mystery men among other Algonkin tribes have pieces of birch bark upon which they scratch rude pictures, each of which reminds them of the first words of the different verses in their songs. Such reminders are great helps to the memory. Among the Iroquois and some eastern Algonkins, they used, as we shall see, wampum belts to help remember the details of treaties or of important events.

Among many tribes pictures were used for recording matters of importance. Many Sioux chiefs have written the story of their life in pictures. They took several large sheets of paper and gummed the edges together so as to make one long strip. Upon this they made pictures representing the important incidents in their lives. Thus in one picture was shown where, as a boy, the artist shot his first deer; in another was represented his first hunting party; in another, how he went on the war-path to gain the name of brave; in another, where he danced the sun dance; again, how he went to Washington to see the white men's officers, on business.

The most important record made by the Sioux is the *Dakota Calendar*. More than a century ago a Sioux Indian determined to keep a count of the years and of their happenings. So he began a record which was called a "winter count," where the events of the different years were shown by pictures. His idea became popular, and a number of these winter counts were begun by other Indians. The most important of these is one which has been called the Dakota Calendar. It belonged for a long time to an Indian named Lone Dog. The one he had was a copy on cloth from a still older one, which had been made upon a buffalo skin. This count appears to have begun about the year 1800.

Each year its maker selected some important event, by which the year was to be remembered, and made a picture for it. The first five or six pictures run in a nearly straight line to the left; the line of pictures then coils around and around this, the last picture always being added to the end of the coiled line. The pictures are in black and red, and while rudely drawn, most of them can be easily recognized. In 1801 the

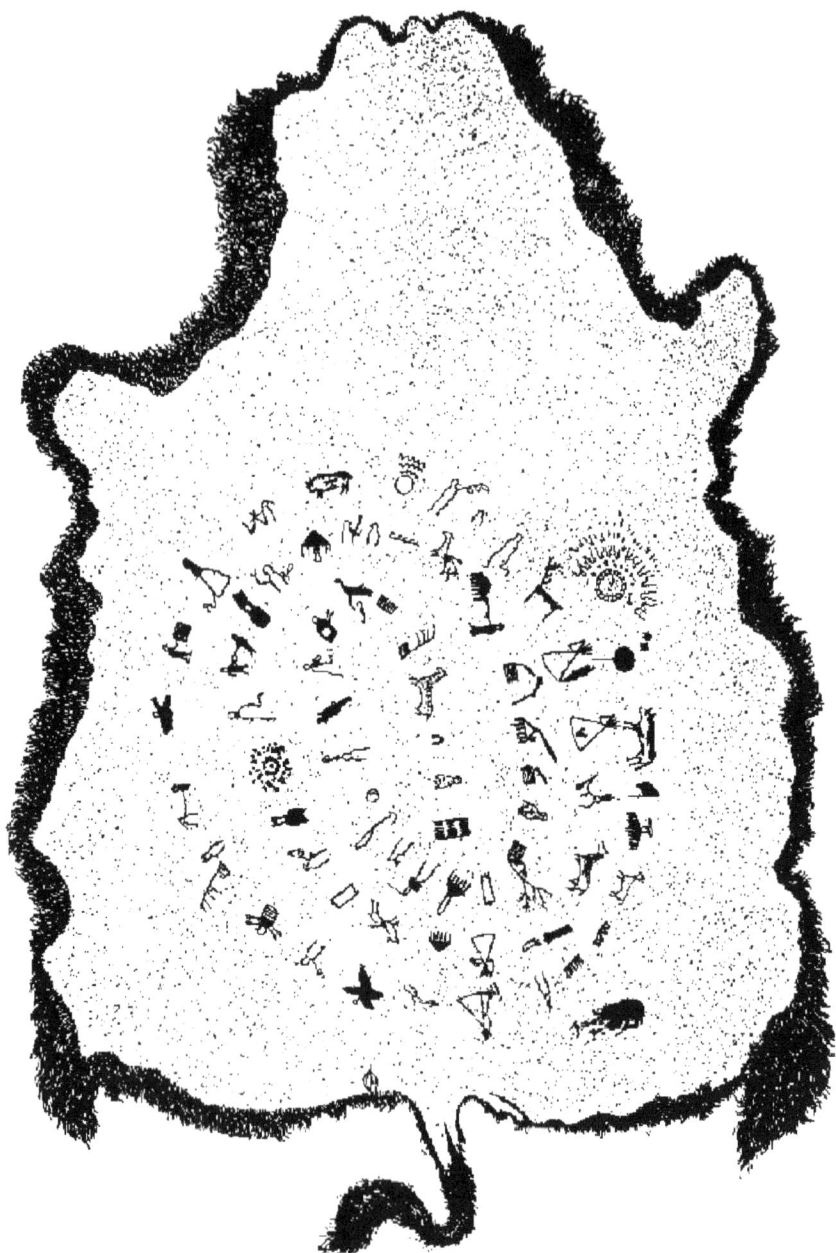

THE DAKOTA CALENDAR. (AFTER MALLERY.)

Sioux had a terrible attack of smallpox, and many of them died; the picture for the year is a man covered with red spots. Whooping-cough is a disease of which white people have little fear, but it is sometimes very destructive to Indians; in 1813 it was among the Sioux, and the picture for that year was a man coughing, as shown by lines diverging from in front of his mouth. In 1840 the Sioux made a treaty of peace with the Cheyennes; the picture shows two hands extended for a friendly grasp. In 1869 there was a total eclipse of the sun, which is represented by a blackened sun and two stars in red: "The stars were seen in the daytime." In 1833 was the famous display of meteors or falling stars, which was witnessed in all parts of the United States, causing great excitement; many white people believed that it portended the destruction of the world. This star shower was noticed by the Sioux keeper of the winter count, and is represented by a black moon and a lot of red stars represented as falling. You can pick out these different figures in the picture, which represents Lone Dog's winter count, or the Dakota Calendar as it would look on a buffalo hide.

Probably you have all seen pictures of a birch-bark letter written many years ago by an Ojibwa Indian. It was written by one of Schoolcraft's guides. Mr. Schoolcraft, with a party of assistants and soldiers, was on a journey of exploration in the Northwest. One morning as they were leaving camp, Schoolcraft saw an Indian putting a bit of birch bark, upon which he had drawn some pictures in black, into a cleft at the end of a pole. This pole was then stuck slantingly into the ground and three notches were cut in it. When Mr. Schoolcraft asked his guide for an explanation, he said this letter would inform any

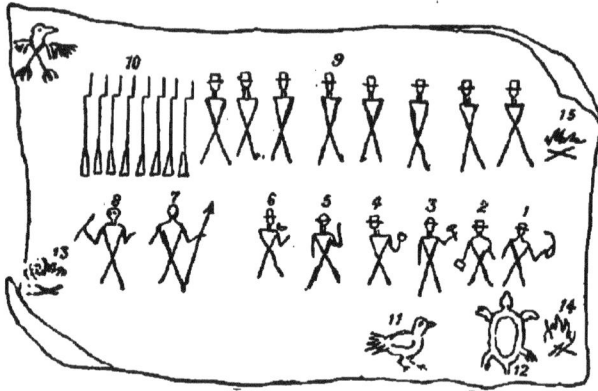

INDIAN LETTER ON BIRCH BARK. (FROM SCHOOLCRAFT.)

Ojibwa Indians who might pass, about their party. The eagle in the upper corner showed that they were from Washington — government people. The other pictures showed that there were eight common soldiers each with a gun; that there were six officers, the duty of each being indicated by something carried in the hand, — the captain by his sword, the secretary by his book, the geologist by his hammer, etc.; that

soldiers and officers were white men, as shown
by their wearing hats; that there were two
guides, Indians, as shown by their having no
hats and carrying spears; that the night before
there were three fires in the camp, soldiers,
officers, and guides, camping separately; that
during the day there had been secured a prairie
hen and a turtle, both of which had been taken
by the officers for supper. But other facts were
shown besides those told in the pictures. The
pole stuck into the ground pointed the direction
in which the party would journey; the three
notches on the pole told that they would journey
in that direction three days.

Of all American Indians those who went
farthest in the direction of developing writing
were some of those living in Mexico and Central
America. The Aztecs had an extensive system
of picture writing. By means of pictures they
recorded their traditional history and gave full
directions regarding the worship of the gods.
They had real books written with these pictures. These books were written sometimes on
skin, sometimes on paper. The Aztecs made
two kinds of paper, one of the soft inner bark of
a tree, the other from the maguey plant. The
latter sort was beaten out of the mass of leaf
fibres after they had been soaked in water. The
maguey plant is much like the century plant
which you have seen in parks and greenhouses.
The paper or dressed skin was made into long

narrow strips many feet in length. These strips
were folded back and forth like a screen, and the
ends were fastened to two thin boards which
served as covers for the book. Sometimes bits
of polished green stone were inlaid into these
covers to make them pretty. Some of these old
books are still in existence, though most of them
have long been destroyed. We cannot read any
of them very well because pictures are uncertain

PAGE OF AZTEC BOOK. (FROM PHOTOGRAPH.)

means of conveying information. Still we can
tell something about their meaning.

The viceroy Mendoza, the first one sent from
Spain to govern Mexico, was greatly interested
in these Mexican books. He wanted his master,
the Emperer Charles V, to know about them,
and ordered three skilled painters of the Aztecs
to prepare a book to be sent to the Emperor.
Each artist took a different subject, so the book

consists of three parts. The first gives a picture-written story of the Aztecs from the time when they began their wanderings; the second gives a list of the towns that paid tribute to the city of Mexico and a statement of the kind and amount of tribute each paid; the third shows how children were trained, how they were punished when they were naughty, and what kind of work they were taught. Of course the Emperor would not understand the meaning of all these queer pictures, far different from anything he had ever seen; so Mendoza had an explanation or translation written with all the pictures. This is as fortunate for us as it was for the Emperor: in this way we can learn something about the use and meaning of these characters.

XI.

MONEY.

INDIANS have always been fond of beads and of shells. Wampum is shell beads of an especial shape — cylindrical, with square cut ends, and with a length one and a half times their thickness or more. This wampum was made from a thick and heavy sea-shell. A piece was split off, and then ground down until it was like a wheat straw in shape and size. It was then cut into lengths and drilled. The drilling was slow and tedious work. A point of stone, or, after the whites came, of metal, was struck into a cane or reed. The bit of shell to be drilled was held in the left hand; the drill was rolled on the thigh with the right hand. There were two kinds of wampum — white and purple. The purple was most valued. Thomas Morton quaintly wrote in 1630 — that is, it sounds quaint to us now, — " White with them is as silver with us, the other as our gould."

Originally wampum was simply ornamental. But it is always easy for things that are prized as ornament to be used in trade. So wampum was used as a medium of exchange; it was really the money of the eastern Indians. Strings of it passed from hand to hand as coin does with us. Sometimes the ornamental string worn a moment before would be removed to buy some object seen and desired. The famous New England chief, King Philip, is said to have had a coat "made all of *wampampeog*, which when in. need of money, he cuts to pieces and distributes it plentifully."

Among the Algonkin and Iroquois tribes broad belts or bands of wampum were neatly woven. The work consisted, like all weaving, of two sets of threads. The long warp threads were crossed by threads laden with beads. These belts were neat and handsome and often contained thousands of beads. The differently colored beads were so combined as to make striking designs and figures.

These fine belts were often given as pledges of faith and agreement at the making of treaties. Some which were kept in the tribe were made to help in remembering the terms of the treaty. Thus, when an orator was speaking, he would hold up a wampum belt, and in making a point of special importance would call attention to some figure in the belt, which would serve ever after to remind every one present of what he had said. Among the Onondagas (Iroquois) there

WAMPUM BELT. (AFTER HOLMES.)

was an officer known as the "keeper of the belts," whose business it was to know all these figures and the different ideas connected with them, and to make them known to the people from time to time.

There is a common little sea-shell found in the Pacific Ocean called the dentalium. It is pretty, clear white, very smooth, and shaped much like a wee elephant's tusk. The natives of the coast are fond of it as ornament, and among them strings of dentalium shells serve for money just as wampum did in the east. They were secured usually by a peculiar mode of fishing. Thus we are told at Forward Inlet a number of split sticks or twigs were tied together into a bunch; this was tied to the end of several poles lashed together so as to reach the bottom in deep water. It was driven down into the mud, and then brought up with the shells caught or tangled in it. The value of the shells depended on their length. Little ones were good enough to be worn as ornaments, but the larger they were, the more value they had as money. Powers, speaking of the Hupa (California) Indians, says: "The standard of measurement is a string of five shells. Nearly every man has ten lines tattooed across the inside of his left arm about half way between the wrist and the elbow; and in measuring shell-money he takes the string in his right hand, draws one end over his left thumb-nail, and if the other end reaches to the uppermost of the tattoo lines, the five shells are worth $25 in gold, or $5 a shell. Of course it is only one in ten thousand that is long enough to reach this high value. The longest ones usually seen are worth about $2, that is $10 to the string. Single shells are also measured on the creases on the inside of the left middle finger, a $5 shell being one which will reach between the two extreme creases. No shell is treated as money at all unless it is long enough to rate at 25 cents. Below that it degenerates into *squaw money*, and goes to form part of a woman's necklace."

Shell beads are much prized among the Pueblo

Indians, and are sometimes in size and shape very like true wampum. At other times they are thin, flat, rather broad pierced disks. These Indians also delight in ornaments made out of haliotis or " abalone " shell. This shell is a large single valve, shaped a little like the ear of some large animal, and hence sometimes called " ear-shell." The outside is rough and unattractive, but the interior is pearly and of rich colors, — purple, green, blue, red, crimson, often many of these bright colors showing in a small space. Where the rough outside of the shell is ground away the whole material is found to be pearly and rich in color. This shell is cut into elliptical, oblong, or fancifully formed plates which are pierced and hung by a cord. Men used to make long journeys to the Pacific Coast to secure shells. Even from the eastern pueblos on the Rio Grande such journeys were customary, and many of the men at Cochiti delight to tell of their journey, perhaps the most important event of their lives. They loaded their burros with things to trade and with supplies, and then struck across a country, desert and hostile, in the hope of bringing back a great load of the precious shell material.

For another precious material they had not far to go. Turquoise was highly prized. This is a hard, fine-grained blue, bluish green, or green stone, that is found at several localities in New Mexico. It has been mined for a long time near

Los Cerillos, and the old diggings and the old stone tools with which they were worked may still be seen. Modern Indians still work the same precious veins, and bits of the rough stone may pass from hand to hand in trade. In drilling the shell and turquoise beads to-day a little drill is used which is called a pump-drill. An upright stick bears a point of hard stone or iron at the bottom. This passes through a hole in a little flat board an inch or so wide and six or eight inches long; strings or thongs pass from the ends of this board to the top of the upright stick. On the upright stick, not far from the lower end, is fastened a thin, wide disk of wood, three inches across. This serves as a fly-wheel to regulate the whirling of the stick. When this little machine is properly adjusted, it is made to whirl by pressing down on the crossbow, and then releasing the pressure, pressing down again, etc. It works very well, and drills the hard turquoise and the softer shell neatly. These beads and ornaments of shell or turquoise are so highly prized that they easily serve the purposes of trade. So much do the Navajo desire the turquoise that they readily exchange for it their beautiful blankets, neat silver-work, or finest ponies.

Blankets have always been greatly prized by all Indians, whether they be made out of skins, bark, or wool. The white man has taken advantage of this fact, and to-day his blankets are to be found everywhere. In some places they have become the real money and have regular set values. In British Columbia, most of the tribes reckon all values in Hudson Bay blankets. These blankets are traded out by the Hudson Bay company and are of various sizes. These sizes are always indicated by some black lines worked into the blanket along the edge. The largest size is called a "four point," the smallest a "one point" blanket. One size is considered the standard; it is the "two-and-a-half point" size. When any one speaks of "a blanket," a two-and-a-half point blanket is meant. Skins of different animals are said to be worth so many "blankets."

The Tlingit and Haida Indians of Alaska and Queen Charlotte Islands used to feel very proud if they were owners of "coppers." They did not smelt copper, but they used to beat it into various forms. The form most prized, called "a copper," was of no use, but indicated wealth. "Coppers" were flat sheets of equal thickness throughout except at the edges, which were thicker than the body; there was also upon them a raised pattern something like a T; sometimes also a face was scratched upon their upper part. Such coppers were formerly worth ten slaves each. Lately, however, the whites have taken to making them for trade, and they have become so common that they are much less prized. Still, until quite lately, they were worth from forty to eighty blankets, or from sixty to one hundred and twenty dollars.

WILLIAM HENRY HOLMES. — Geologist, archæologist, artist. At present he is at the head of the anthropological work of the United States National Museum. Has written important works : among them, *Art in Shell of the Ancient Americans* and *Archæological Studies among the Ancient Cities of Mexico.*

XII.

MEDICINE MEN AND SECRET SOCIETIES.

ALL Indians believe in spirits. Some are good and help men who please them; others are bad and always anxious to do harm. The spirits are all about us. They are in plants, and trees, and rustling leaves; they are in the wind and cloud and rain; they are in the mountain and in the brook. It is spirits that cause trouble, suffering, and death. When a man is ill, some bad spirit has taken away his soul or has entered into him.

It is not strange, then, that the Indians should wish to gain power over these spirits. If a man knows some words, the saying of which will protect him against them, he is fortunate; fortunate is he, too, if he knows some object which, carried, will disarm them, or if he can perform some trick which will put them to flight. Such knowledge is what the Indians mean by "medicine" or "mystery." Men who spend their lives in trying to gain such knowledge are called medicine men, mystery men, or Shamans.

The Shaman among the tribes of the Northwest

Coast is an important person. He decided, when a boy, that he would become a Shaman. He selected some old Shaman for his teacher and learned from him his secrets. By experiments,

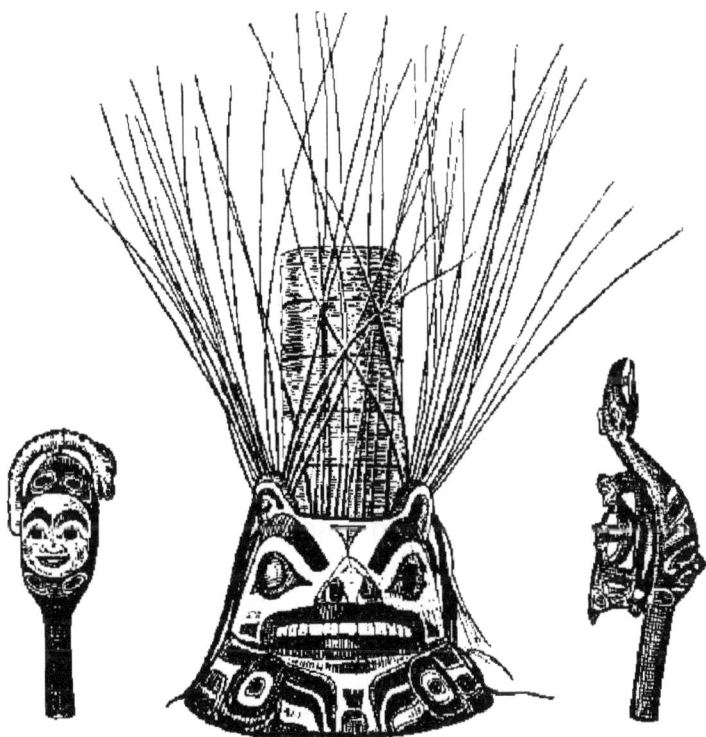

RATTLES AND MASKS: ALASKA. (FROM ORIGINALS IN PEABODY MUSEUM.)

by dreaming, and by trading with other Shamans he got other secrets. To help him in his dealings with spirits the Shaman makes use of many devices. He sleeps upon a wooden pillow, which is carved with otter heads; these are believed to

whisper wisdom to him while he sleeps. Upon
his dancing-dress little carved figures, in ivory,
are hung, which give him spirit influence, partly
by the forms into which they are cut, and partly
by the jingling noise they make when he dances.
He wears a mask, the animal carvings on which
control spirits. He uses a rattle and a tambourine
to summon spirits. He has a spirit pole or wand
quaintly carved, with which he fences, fighting
and warding off spirits which he alone can see.
The people sitting by see his brave fighting and
hear his shrieks and cries; in this way only they
can judge how many and how powerful are the
spirits against whom he is fighting, for their
good.

Sometimes when dancing the Shaman becomes
so excited that he falls in a fit — quivering, gasp-
ing, struggling. It is believed, at such times,
either that some mighty spirit has taken possession of him, or that his own soul has gone to the
land of spirits. Sometimes when he comes to
himself he tells of his wonderful journeys and
battles.

Among the Haida of the Queen Charlotte
Islands, when a sick man is to be cured, three or
four Shamans come together at his side. All
sing and rattle until they find out where the soul
of the sick man is. It may be in the possession
of the salmon or the oolachen fish, or it may be
held a prisoner by some dead Shaman. They go
to the place where it is supposed to be, and by

singing and charms succeed in getting it into a carved hollow bone used only for this purpose. Various precious things are then burned and the soul bone held in the smoke. The bone is then laid by the side of the patient's head that his soul may return.

Many astonishing stories are told of the powers of medicine men. A missionary among the Crees, Edgerton R. Young, told me of a white man who was once out hunting. He came upon an old medicine man, who begged him for game, as he was hungry. The white man made sport of him, saying, " You are a great medicine man ; why not get game for yourself ? " The old man was enraged. He cried out, " White man, see yonder goose," and pointed his finger into the air. The goose fell fluttering at their feet, and the old man picked it up and walked away. The white man really thought this thing happened. Perhaps the old medicine man had hypnotized him; if so, the only goose anywhere around was probably the white man.

The eastern Algonkins were fond of medicine or mystery. Two great medicine men would have a contest to see which was more powerful. Many of their stories tell of such contests. Two powers, which they did seem to have, attracted much attention and caused much terror. These were screaming and sinking into the ground. Leland quotes an Indian regarding these: " Two or three weeks after, I was in another place, we spoke of *m'teoulin* [mystery men]. The white folks ridiculed them. I said there was one in Fredericton, and I said I would bet ten dollars that he would get the better of them. And they bet that no Indian could do more than they could. So the *m'teoulin* came, and first he screamed so that no one could move. It was dreadful. Then he took seven steps through the ground up to his ankles, just as if it had been light snow. When I asked for the ten dollars, the white men paid."

Ojibwa medicine men have often been tested by white men who doubted their powers. Thus one old medicine man had two little houses built at some distance apart. He was shut up in one, and the whites built a ring of fire around it. Then, no one could tell how, he appeared un-harmed walking out of the *other* house. These things are no doubt tricks or delusions, but the medicine man's apparent ability to do them greatly increased his influence among the people.

Much use is made of words as charms and of sacred numbers. Four and seven are sacred numbers among the Cherokees. Once, wishing to see his method of curing disease, I asked the old medicine man to treat my lame arm. He sent out for four kinds of leaves, which were to be fresh and young, and one other sort which was to be dry and dead. The latter had little thorns along its edges. The old man pounded up the four kinds in warm water. He then scratched the arm with the other, nearly drawing blood. The arm was rubbed with the bruised leaves. The medicine man then blew upon my arm seven times. He went through this operation of rubbing and blowing four times, thus combining the numbers four and seven. He repeated charms all the time as he rubbed.

The Shaman does business as an individual. He expects pay from those who employ him. His knowledge and power over spirits is individual and for individuals. Among some tribes we find not single medicine men, but great secret societies which have learned spirit wisdom to use for the benefit of the society, or for the good of the whole tribe. Such secret societies are notable in the Southwest — and elsewhere. They may work to cure disease in individuals; they also work for the whole tribe. Among the Moki Pueblos, the societies of the Snake and of the Antelope carry on the snake dance, that the whole people may have rain for their fields.

XIII.

DANCES AND CEREMONIALS.

THE dances of Indians are sometimes, like our own, simply social and for pleasure. They are more frequently religious or for some important purpose.

They are always accompanied by music. Indian music is in perfect swing or time. Most
Indian musical instruments are simply time
beaters. The commonest is the rattle. This
varies with place and tribe. Among Northwest
Coast tribes it is of wood, elaborately carved,
both in form and decoration. A common rattle
in that district is cut into the form of a bird —
the raven. Some of the old rattles, made and
used by Shamans a hundred years ago, are still
in existence: they were probably carved with
knives and chisels of stone, but they are better
done than most of the modern ones, which have
been cut out with metal tools. Some of the
Plains tribes had leather rattles, — balls of dried
skin fastened over the end of a little wooden
handle. Many tribes used gourds for rattles.
Some of these are round, about the size of an
apple; such were pierced and a wooden handle
thrust through. Others are flask or bottle
shaped; such need no handle beyond the one
supplied by nature.

Drums and tambourines of various kinds are
used in time beating. The beaters usually take
no other part in the dance, but sit by themselves
at one side. Frequently each dancer has a rattle. Sometimes a stick notched across with
deep notches is used. Across these notches a
thin bone, usually a shoulder-blade, is rubbed
with a good deal of force. Such rubbed sticks
are very good time beaters. They are used by

Apaches, Pueblos, and Tonkaways. Among the old Aztecs, they had a similar instrument, but made of a long bone instead of from a stick.

Indians prepare for dances with much care. The hair is combed and arranged. The face and body are painted. A special dance dress is frequently worn. This dress is often of ancient form and decoration. Sometimes all this preparation is just to make the dancers look pretty; more frequently, however, the dress and decoration have some meaning, and often they mimic some creature or copy the dress worn by some great person of their legends. Thus in the buffalo and the bear dances, skins of buffalo, with the head, skin, and horns attached, or the skins of bears, were put on, to make the dancers look like these animals.

The meaning and uses of dances differ greatly. The war dance, in which the men are painted as if for war and have about them everything that can make them think of war, is intended to influence them for battle. The music, songs, movements, prayers, and offerings all relate to the coming conflict. The scalp dance is in celebration of victory. The buffalo dance is magical and is to compel the coming of herds of that animal. At some dances the story told by the tribe in regard to the creation of the world and how man learned things is all acted out; the dancers are dressed to represent the spirits, or beings who made, helped, or taught

the tribe, and the dance is a real drama. Among
the Pueblos and some other southwestern tribes,
many dances are prayers for rain; the songs sung
and the movements made all have reference to the
rain so much desired.

In one of these dances the drummers make
curious, beckoning gestures to bring up the
rain clouds. In some the dancers carry sticks
curiously jointed together so as to open and
shut in zigzag movements, which are meant to
look like lightning and are believed to bring
it; other dancers imitate the thunder. Sometimes the dancers and others are drenched with
water thrown upon them, in order that the town
and its fields may be drenched with rain.

Many dances were only a part of some great
religious ceremonial. Thus the sun dance follows several days of fasting and prayer, and the
snake dance is but a small part of a nine days'
ceremonial. Indian religion abounds in such
long ceremonials with a vast number of minute
details. The songs, prayers, and significant ac-
tions used in some of them must number many
hundreds.

In order that the desired result of ceremonials
should be secured, it was necessary that the persons performing it should be pure. There were
many ways to purify or cleanse oneself. Sometimes a sweat bath was taken, after which the body
was rubbed with sweet-smelling plants. The person might sit in smoke that came from burning

some sacred herb or wood. He might fast for several days. He might refuse to touch or come into contact with his friends, or with the objects he was in the habit of using. Many times it was thought necessary that the objects which he was to use in the ceremony must be new, or must be purified by being held in sacred smoke.

In ceremonies, much attention is paid to sacred numbers. The number most often sacred is four. Four men are often concerned in one act; four drums may be used; the men may fast four days; an action may be repeated four times. If a thing is done sixteen times, four times four, it might be still better. In the snake-dance ceremonial there are sixteen sacred songs, which are sung at one sitting.

Seven is a sacred number among the Cherokees; it is less important than four, but the two may be combined, and twenty-eight often occurs. Thus the scratcher upon the ball-players has seven teeth and is drawn four times, making twenty-eight scratches.

Connected with the sacred number four, the Indians give much importance to the cardinal points — north, west, south, and east. They always pay attention to these when they dance and pray. Some tribes recognize more than four world's points, adding the up and the down, or the above and the below, making six in all. A few think of the place where they themselves are, and speak of seven points; so the Zuñi have the north, west, south, east, above, below, and the center. When they prepared their medicine lodge for the sun dance, the Mandans put one of their curious, turtle-shaped, skin water-drums at each of the four world quarters. Usually in ceremonials, Indians pray to each of these quarters, and make an offering toward it.

One of the commonest offerings made in ceremonials is the smoke of tobacco. Gods and spirits are believed to be fond of it. In smoking to their honor, a puff is blown in turn to each of the four points, and then perhaps up, and possibly down. In the Pueblos, every religious act is accompanied by the scattering of sacred meal. This sacred meal is a mixture of corn meal and pounded sea-shells. It is sprinkled everywhere to secure kindly spirit influence. A pinch of it is thrown to the north, west, south, east, up and down. Frank Cushing once took a party of Zuñi Indians to the Atlantic Ocean to get sea-water for certain ceremonials. On the way, the Indians saw many novel and strange things which they did not understand. When they saw such, they sprinkled sacred meal to render them harmless and kindly.

Prayer sticks are much used among the Pueblos. They are bits of stick to which feathers are attached. They are set up wherever it is desired to have the good will of spirit powers. For several days before the Moki snake dance, messengers are sent out with prayer sticks to be set

up near springs and sacred places. Such prayer
sticks are put up near fields where corn is planted,
or buried in the earth in corrals where ponies or
burros are kept. Other offerings are made at especially sacred spots. In mountain caves there
are often masses of prayer sticks, miniature bows
and arrows, and other tiny things meant as gifts
to the gods.

Each of the cardinal points may have a color
that is proper to it. The use of sacred colors for
the cardinal points is found among the Pueblos,
Navajo, many Siouan tribes, the Pani, and others.
It was the custom also among the old Aztecs in
Mexico. A curious example of the use of these
colors is found in the sand altars of the Pueblos
and Navajo. They are made in many ceremonials. They are made of different colored sands
produced by pounding up rocks. The sand altars are rectangular in form, and are made on the
floor. A layer of one color of sand may be spread
out for a foundation; upon it may be put a sheet
of sand of a different color and of smaller size, so
that the margin of the first serves as a border of
the second; additional layers may be added, each
bordering the one that follows it. Finally, upon
the topmost layer, curious and interesting designs
may be made. One sand altar in the Moki snake
dance had an outer broad border of brownish
yellow sand; then followed broad borders of white
and black; upon this black border were four
snakes in red, green, yellow, and blue, one on each

side of the square; then came narrower borders
of white, red, green, yellow, one within the other;
within these was a central square of green, upon
which was a yellow mountain lion.

You see that Indian ceremonials are often very
complex, with many dances, decorations, purify-
ings, prayers, gifts, and altars.

XIV.

BURIAL AND GRAVES.

ALMOST all savage and barbarous peoples look
upon death as due to bad spirits, to witchcraft, or
to violence. They cannot realize that men should
die of old age. Disease is generally thought to
be due to bad spirits or to the influence of some
medicine man.

After a man dies there are many ways of treating the body. Usually the face is painted almost
as if the person were preparing for a feast or a
dance. The Otoes and many other tribes dress
out the body in its choicest clothing and finest
ornaments.

Probably burial in the ground is the commonest way of disposing of the dead body. The
exact method varies. The grave may be deep, or
it may be so shallow as hardly to be a grave at
all. The body may be laid in extended to its
full length, or it may be bent and folded together

into the smallest possible space, and tied securely in this way. Great attention is frequently given to the direction toward which the face or the body is turned. Among some tribes it makes no difference whether the earth touches the body; in others the greatest care is taken to prevent this.

The Sacs and Foxes in Iowa have their graveyards on the side of a hill, high above the surrounding country. The graves are shallow; the body, wrapped in blankets, is laid out at full length; little, if any, earth is thrown directly upon the body, but a little arched covering made of poles laid side by side, lengthwise of the body, is built over it, and a little earth may be thrown upon it. A pole is set at the head of the grave to the top of which is hung a bit of rag or a little cloth, the flapping of which, perhaps, keeps off bad spirits. Various objects are laid upon the grave: for men, bottles, and perhaps knives; for women, buckets and pans, such as are used in their daily work; for little children, the baby-boards on which they used to lie, and the little toys of which they were fond.

Sometimes grave-boxes were made of slabs of stone. Such are known in various parts of the United States, but are most common in Tennessee, where ancient cemeteries, with hundreds of such graves, are known. (See XV. Mounds and their Builders.) Sometimes the bodies of those lately dead were buried in these, but sometimes there were placed in them the dry bones of people long dead, who had been buried elsewhere, or whose bodies had been exposed for a time on scaffolds or in dead-houses. Among several northeastern tribes it was the custom to place the bodies for some time in dead-houses, or temporary graves, and at certain times to collect together all the bones, and bury them at once in some. great trench or hole.

Most tribes buried objects with the dead. With a man were buried his bow and arrows, war-club, and choicest treasures. The woman was accompanied by her ornaments, tools, and uten-sils. Even the child had with it its little toys and cradle, as we have seen in connection with the Sacs and Foxes. The Indians believed that people have souls which live somewhere after the men die. These souls hereafter delight to do the same things the men did here. There they hunt, and fish, and war, work and play, eat and drink. So weapons and tools, food and drink, were placed with the body in the grave.

They knew perfectly well that the *things* do not go away; they believed, however, that things have souls, as men do, and that it is the soul of the things that goes with the soul of the man into the land of spirits. Among tribes that are great horsemen, like the Comanches, a man's ponies are killed at his death. His favorite horse, decked out in all his trappings, is killed at the grave, so that the master may go properly mounted. When a little child among the Sacs and Foxes dies, a little dog is killed at the grave to accompany the child soul, and help the poor little one to find its way to the spirit world. Such destruction or burial of property may be very nice for the dead man's soul, but it is not nice for the man's survivors, who are sometimes quite beggared by it.

Sometimes the objects put into or upon a grave are broken, pierced, or bent. The purpose in thus making the objects "dead" has sometimes been said to be to set free the soul of the object; far more frequently, it is likely that it is to prevent bad persons robbing the grave for its treasures.

Cremation or burning the dead body was found among a number of Indian tribes, particularly upon the Pacific Coast. The Senel in California and some Oregon tribes are among these. So are the Tlingit of Alaska and their near neighbors and kin, the Haida of Queen Charlotte Islands. Among the last two tribes all but the Shamans were usually burned. The Shamans were buried in boxes raised on tall posts. After a Tlingit or Haida body was burned the ashes were usually gathered and placed in a little box-like cavity excavated in an upright post near its base; at the top of this post was a cross-board on which was carved or painted the *totem* or crest of the dead man.

Where there were great caves (as in Kentucky), and where the people dwelt in caverns (as at one time in the Southwest), the dead were often laid

away in some corner of the cave. In almos
such cases the body was folded into the sr
est space, with the knees drawn up against
chin; it was then wrapped up in blankets
robes and corded. Such bodies were genei
not buried, but simply stowed away. These d
bodies are sometimes called " mummies," but
name should only be used when something

SCAFFOLD BURIAL. (AFTER YARROW.)

been done to the body with the definite purj
of preserving it.

Mention has already been made of box bi
in connection with the Tlingit and Haida
mans. Many Eskimos bury their dead in b
supported on posts. The weapons, tools,
utensils of the dead are usually stuck upon
posts or hung over the boxes. The Ponkas

bury in raised boxes, and at their present reservation in Oklahoma there are two extensive cemeteries of this kind.

Among some tribes in the extreme north-
western part of the United States canoes are
used instead of boxes. They are supported
above ground by posts. Usually two canoes are
used; the body is placed in the lower, larger one;
the smaller one is turned upside down over the
corpse and fits within the larger. In the Mississippi and Missouri valley region many Siouan
tribes placed their dead upon scaffolds, supported
by poles at a height of six or eight feet in the air.
Extensive cemeteries of this kind used to occupy
high points overlooking the rivers; they could
be seen — dreary sights — a long way across the
country. Some tribes in wooded districts placed
the dead in trees. Often scaffold and tree burial
were only temporary, the body being later taken
elsewhere for permanent burial. One time, visiting a winter camp of the Sacs and Foxes, far
from their permanent village, we saw a strange
bundle in a tree. It was the blanketed corpse of
an old woman who had died a few days before;
the party took it with them when they returned
home in the spring.

We should find some of the mourning customs
interesting. The friends of the dead wail and
scream fearfully; they cut off their hair; they
gash their bodies; they sometimes even chop off
their finger tips or whole joints. They watch by

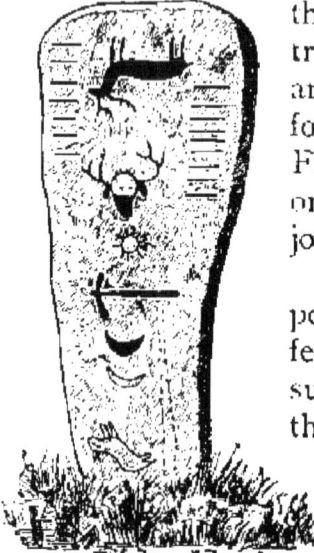

OJIBWA GRAVEPOST. (FROM SCHOOLCRAFT.)

the grave — this is particularly true of women. Food and drink are often carried to the grave for some time after the burial. Fires are kindled to supply light or heat to the soul on its long journey.

Not many tribes have special posts or marks at the grave. A few do. The Ojibwa made such with much care. Usually they bore pictures or marks telling about the dead man. His totem animal was often represented, usually upside down to indicate that the bearer of the emblem was dead.

H. C. YARROW. — Army physician, ethnologist. Wrote, among other papers, *A Further Contribution to the Study of the Mortuary Customs of the North American Indians.*

XV.

MOUNDS AND THEIR BUILDERS.

IN many parts of the United States, from western New York to the Rocky Mountains and even beyond, there are great numbers of artificial heaps and extensive embankments of earth.

These show skill in construction, and from them have been dug many relics of artistic merit and good workmanship. At one time these earthworks and relics were generally believed to be the work of a single, highly civilized people, who preceded the Indians, who were not related to them, and who are now extinct. To this people the name "mound-builders" was given.

There are three ways in which we can learn about these so-called "mound-builders." We may learn something from the mounds themselves, from the relics found in the mounds, and from the bones of persons who were buried in them.

Studying the mounds themselves, we find that they differ in different areas. We will look at three areas:

(1) In Ohio there are thousands of mounds and earthworks. Near every important modern town there are groups of them. Cincinnati, Chillicothe, Dayton, Xenia, are all near important mounds.

The regular enclosures are numerous in this area: these are great embankments of earth inclosing a regular space. Some are in the form of circles; others are four-sided; in a few cases they are eight-sided. Sometimes a square and a circle are united. There is one such combination at Hopeton; one of the embankments is a nearly true circle containing twenty acres; joined to it is a square of almost the same area.

At Newark there was a wonderful group of enclosures. The group covered about two miles square and consisted of three divisions, which were connected with one another by long parallel embankment walls. One circle in this group contained more than thirty acres: the walls were twelve feet high and fifty feet wide; a ditch seven feet deep and thirty-five feet wide bordered it on the inner side; a gap of eighty feet in the circle served as an entrance. In the center of the area enclosed by this great circle was a curious earth heap somewhat like a bird in form. Northwest from this great circle, nearly a mile distant, were two connected enclosures, one octagonal, the other circular: the former contained more than fifty acres, the latter twenty. East from these and northeast from the great circle was a fine twenty-acre enclosure, nearly a square in form. Besides these great walls, there were long parallel lines of connecting embankment walls, small circular enclosures, and little mounds in considerable variety. This great mass of works represented an enormous amount of time and labor.

What was the purpose of these regular enclosures? Some writers claim that they were forts for protection; others consider them protections for the corn-fields; others think they were places for games or religious ceremonials; one eminent man insists that they were foundations upon which were built long and narrow houses.

"Altar mounds" occur in Ohio. Professor

Putnam and his assistants opened a number of these. They are small, rounded heaps of earth. At their center is a basin-shaped mass of hard clay showing the effect of fire. These basins are a yard or four feet across and contain ashes and charcoal. Upon these are found many curious objects. On one altar were two bushels of ornaments made of stone, copper, mica, shells, bears' teeth, and sixty thousand pearls. Most of these objects were pierced with a small hole and were apparently strung as ornaments. These objects had all been thrown into a fire- blazing on the altar and had been spoiled by the heat. After the kindling of the fire, and the destruction of these precious things, earth had been heaped up over. the altars, completing the mound.

The most famous mound in Ohio is *the great serpent* in Adams County. It lies upon a narrow ridge between three streams, which unite. It is a gigantic serpent form made in earth; across the widely opened jaws it measures seventy-five feet; the body, just behind the head, measures thirty feet across and five feet high; following the curves the length is thirteen hundred forty-eight feet. The tail is thrown into a triple coil. In front of the serpent is an elliptical enclosure with a heap of stones at its center. Beyond this is a form, somewhat indistinct, thought by some to be a frog. Probably this wonderful earthwork was connected with some old religion. While there are many other earthworks of other forms in Ohio, the *sacred enclosures*, the *altar mounds*, and the *great serpent* are the most characteristic.

(2) In Wisconsin the most interesting mounds are the *effigy mounds*. There are great numbers of them in parts of this and a few adjoining states.

GREAT SERPENT MOUND: OHIO. (FROM THE CENTURY MAGAZINE.)

They are earthen forms of mammals, birds, and reptiles. They are usually in groups; they are generally well shaped and of gigantic size. Among the quadrupeds represented are the buffalo, moose, elk, deer, fox, wolf, panther, and lynx. Mr. Peet, who has carefully studied them, shows that quadruped mammals are always represented in profile so that only two legs are shown; the birds have their wings spread; reptiles sprawl, showing all four legs; fish are mere bodies without limbs. We have said these earth pictures are gigantic: some panthers have tails three hundred and fifty feet long, and some eagles measure one thousand feet from tip to tip of the outspread wings. Not only are these great animal and bird pictures found in Wisconsin in relief; occasionally they are found cut or sunken in the soil. With these curious effigy mounds there occur hundreds of simple burial mounds.

The purpose of the effigy mounds is somewhat uncertain. Some authors think they represent the totem animals after which the families of their builders were named, and that they served as objects of worship or as guardians over the villages.

(3) Farther south, in western Tennessee, another class of mounds is common. These contain graves made of slabs of stone set on edge. The simplest of these stone graves consist of six stones: two sides, two ends, one top, and one bottom. There may be a single one of these graves in a mound, or there may be many. In one mound, about twelve miles from Nashville, which was forty-five feet across and twelve feet high, were found about one hundred skeletons, mostly in stone graves, which were in ranges, one above another. The upper graves contained the

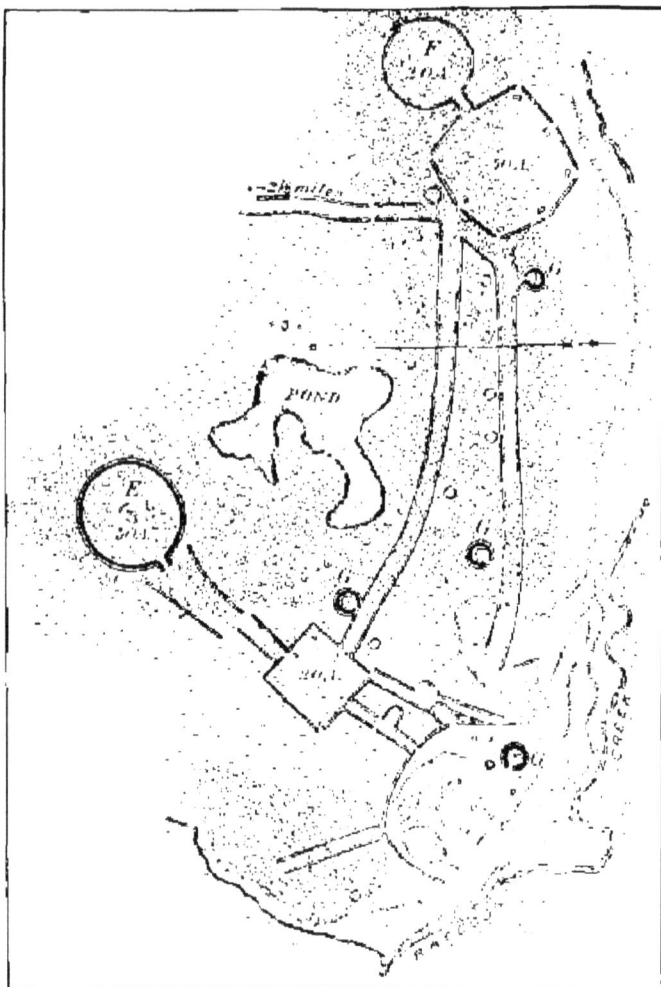

GROUND PLAN OF EARTHWORKS AT NEWARK, OHIO. (AFTER SQUIER
AND DAVIS.)

bones of bodies, which had been buried stretched at full length; the bones were found in their natural positions.   The lower graves were short and square, and the bones in them had been cleaned and piled up in little heaps.   This mound was very carefully made.   The lids of the upper graves were so arranged as to make a perfectly smooth, rounded surface.   Sometimes these stone graves of Tennessee are not placed in mounds, but in true graveyards in the level fields.   In these stone graves are found beautiful objects of stone, shell, and pottery.   The stone-grave men were true artists in working these materials.

In the same district are found many dirt rings called "house-circles."   These occur in groups and appear to mark the sites of ancient villages, each being the ruin of a house.   These rings are nearly circular and from ten to fifty feet across, and from a few inches to two or three feet high. Excavation within them shows old floors made of hard clay, with the fireplace or hearth.   The stone-grave people lived in these houses.   They often buried little children who died, under the floor. Their stone coffins measured only from one to four feet long.   They contain the little skeletons and all the childish treasures — pretty cups and bowls of pottery, shell beads, pearls, and even the leg bones of birds, on which the babies used to cut their teeth as our babies do on rubber rings.

These are but three of the areas where mounds are found; there are several others.   If the "mound-builders" were a single people, with one set of customs, one language, and one government, it is strange that there should be such great differences in the mounds they built. If we had space to speak about the relics from the mounds, they would tell a story.

They would show that the builders of the mounds, while they made many beautiful things of stone, shell, bone, beaten metals, could not

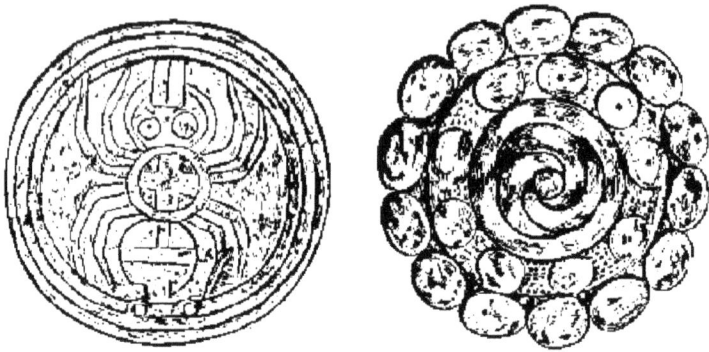

SHELL GORGETS: TENNESSEE. (AFTER HOLMES.)

smelt ores.   They were Stone Age men, not civilized men.   The objects from different areas differ so much in kind, pattern, and material as to suggest that their makers were not one people. Study of skulls from mounds in one district — as Ohio or Iowa — show that different types of men built the mounds even of one area.

So neither the mounds, the relics, nor the remains prove that there was one people, the "mound-builders," but rather that the mounds were built by many different tribes. These tribes were not of civilized, but of barbarous, Stone Age men. It is likely that some of the tribes that built the mounds still live in the United States. Thus the Shawnees may be the descendants of the stone-grave people, the Winnebagoes may have come from the effigy-builders of Wisconsin, and the Cherokees may be the old Ohio " mound-builders."

E. G. SQUIER and E. H. DAVIS. — Authors of *Ancient Monuments of the Mississippi Valley*, published in 1847. It was the *first* great work on American Archæology.

INCREASE ALLEN LAPHAM. — Civil engineer, scientist. His *Antiquities of Wisconsin* was published in 1855.

STEPHEN D. PEET. — Minister, antiquarian, editor. Established *The American Antiquarian*, which he still conducts. Wrote *Emblematic Mounds*.

CYRUS THOMAS. — Minister, entomologist, archæologist. In charge of the mound exploration of the Bureau of Ethnology. Wrote *Burial Mounds of the Northern Sections of the United States* and *Report of the Mound Explorations of the Bureau of Ethnology*.

FREDERIC WARD PUTNAM. — Ichthyologist, archæologist, teacher. For many years Curator of the Peabody Museum of Ethnology, at Cambridge, Mass. Has organized much field work upon mounds of Ohio and Tennessee. Also Curator in Anthropology at the American Museum of Natural History in New York.

XVI.

THE ALGONKINS.

ALGONKIN tribes occupied the Atlantic seacoast from Nova Scotia and New Brunswick south to Virginia, and stretched west as far, at places, as the Rocky Mountains. They also occupied a large area in the interior of British America north of the Great Lakes. Brinton names more than thirty tribes of this great group. Among the best known of these were the Lenape (Delawares), Blackfeet, Ojibwas, and Crees.

It was chiefly Algonkin tribes with whom the first white settlers met. The Indians who supplied the Pilgrims with corn in that first dreadful winter were Algonkins; so were Powhatan and Pocahontas, King Philip and Massasoit. Of course whites came into contact with the Iroquois in New York, and with the Cherokees, the Creeks, and their kin in the south, but much the larger part of their early Indian acquaintance was Algonkin.

There are a number of borrowed Indian words in our English language of to-day. *Wigwam, wampum, squaw, papoose, moccasin,* are examples. These have been taken from the Indian languages into our own, and most of them — all of those mentioned — are Algonkin. They soon became common to English speakers, and were carried by them everywhere they went. All the western tribes had their own names for all these objects, but we have forced these upon them, and to-day we may hear Utes speak of *wig-wams* and Navajo talk about *squaws* or *moccasins*.

We shall speak of two Algonkin tribes. One — the Lenape — is eastern; the other — the Black-feet — is western. The former are woodland, the latter Plains Indians. The Lenape lived in settled villages, and had a good deal of agriculture; they were also hunters, fishermen, and warriors. Their houses were like those of their Iroquois neigh-bors, but each family had its own. They were huts of poles and interwoven branches with a thatching of corn leaves, the stalk of sweet-flag, or the bark of trees. Sometimes at the center of the village, surrounded by the houses, was a sort of hillock or mound from which the country around might be overlooked. The women made good garments of deerskin with skillful beadwork. In cooking they used soapstone vessels. For pounding corn they had mortars of wood, dug out of a section of a tree trunk, and long stone pestles.

In districts where the wild rice or *zizania* grew abundantly great quantities of it were gathered. The women in canoes paddled out among the plants, bent the heads over the edge of the canoe and beat out the grain. This was a food supply of no importance to the Lenape, but the Ojibwas and their neighbors used much of it.

OJIBWA WOMEN GATHERING WILD RICE. (AFTER SCHOOLCRAFT.)

In war, the men used the bow and arrows, spear and tomahawk. They protected themselves with round shields. They speared fish in the streams and lakes or caught them in brush nets or with hooks of bone or bird-claws.

There were three totems of the Lenape. Every man was either a wolf, turkey, or turtle. He had one of these three animals for his emblem, and was as fond of drawing or carving it as a boy among us is of writing his name. This emblem was signed to treaties, it was painted on the houses, it was carved on stones. But only those who were turtles drew their totem entire; usually the wolf or the turkey were represented only by one foot. Between a person and his totem there was a curious friendship, and it was believed that the animal was a sort of protector and friend of those who bore his name. All who had the same totem were blood-relations.

All Algonkins were accustomed to draw pictures to record events. The blankets of chiefs were decorated with such pictures. The Ojibwas were fond of writing birch-bark letters. One of the most interesting Indian records known is the *Walam olum;* this means the red score or red record. Probably it at first consisted of a lot of little sticks or boards with some quaint red pictures upon them. These were probably kept tied together into a little bundle. The original sticks have long been lost, but the one hundred and eighty-four pictures were copied and are still preserved. They were intended to assist in remembering a long poetical legend in which the Algonkin ideas regarding the creation of the world and their tribal history were told.

At first everything was good. Animals and men lived in peace. Then a wicked serpent tried to drown the world. Only a few persons escaped to the back of a great turtle. Their great hero Nanabush helped them. The waters subsided. As the land where they now found themselves was cold, the people determined to move southward. The story of their quarrels and divisions on the journey is told, and also the way in which they seized their new home, destroying or driving out the original owners.

The song in which this story is told is long and full of old words difficult to understand. The Indians themselves must have had difficulty in remembering it. It was a great help to have these little sticks with the red pictures to remind them of its different parts.

Far to the west, close against the base of the Rocky Mountains, lived a famous Algonkin tribe — the Blackfeet. They were great buffalo hunters and warriors. We often think of Indians as being stern and morose, never smiling, never amused. Yet most tribes had sunny tempers like children. Mr. Grinnell, to show this side of Indian nature, describes a day in camp in the olden, happy time. Two parts of his description describe feasts and gambling. Feasts were in constant progress: sometimes one man would give three in a day; men who were favorites might go from feast to feast all day long. If a man wished to give a feast, he ordered the best food he had to be cooked. Then, going outside, he called out the list of invited guests: the name of each one was cried three times. At the close of his invitation he announced how many pipes would be smoked: usually three. When the guests came, each was given a dish, with his share of the food; no one might have a second help, but it was quite polite to carry away what was not eaten.

While the guests were feasting, the man of the house prepared a pipe and tobacco. After the eating was over, the pipe was lighted and passed from hand to hand, each person giving it to the one on his left. Meantime stories of hunting and war were narrated and jokes cracked. Only one man spoke at one time, the rest listening until he was through. Thus they whiled away the time until the last pipe was smoked out, when the host, knocking the ashes from the pipe, told them they might go.

All Indians are gamblers, and they have many gambling games. The Blackfeet played one which was something like the famous game of Chunkey, played among the Creeks. (See XIX.) A wheel about four inches in diameter with five spokes on which were beads of different colors, made of horn or bone, was used. It was rolled

along upon a smooth piece of ground at the ends
of which logs were laid to stop it.   One player
stood at each end of the course.   After a player
set the wheel to rolling, he hurled a dart after it.
This was done just before the wheel reached the
end of its journey.   Points were counted according to the way in which the wheel and dart fell
with reference to each other.   Ten counts made

BLACKFOOT SQUAW TRAVELING.

the game.   This game always attracted great.
crowds of spectators, who became greatly excited
and bet heavily on the result.

At night about their camp-fires the Blackfeet
delighted to tell their sacred stories, which they
did not dare repeat in daylight.   In telling a
story of personal adventure, Indians, like white
people, were often tempted to make it larger than
it really was,

The Blackfeet and some other Indians had the following mode of getting at the truth. When a man told an improbable story some one handed a pipe to the medicine man, who painted the stem red and prayed over it, asking that the man's life might be long if his story were true, but cut short if the story were false. The pipe was then filled and lighted and given to the man. The medicine man said, as he handed it to him: "Accept this pipe, but remember that if you smoke, your story must be as sure as that there is a hole through this pipe and as straight as the hole through this stem. So your life shall be long and you shall survive; but if you have spoken falsely, your days are counted." If he refused to smoke, as he surely would if he had not spoken true things, every one knew that he was a braggart and a liar.

DANIEL GARRISON BRINTON. — Physician, anthropologist. Has written many books, mostly about American Indians. *The Lenape and their Legends*, in which the *Walam olum* is given in full, is a volume in his *Library of Aboriginal American Literature*.

XVII.

THE SIX NATIONS.

WHEN white men began to settle what is now the state of New York, that part of it extending from about the Hudson River west along the

Mohawk and on beyond it to the Niagara, was occupied by the Iroquois or Five Nations. The separate tribes, naming them from the east, were the Mohawks, Oneidas, Onondagas, Cayugas, and Senecas. These were flourishing tribes; they had important villages and towns and large corn-fields; they were, however, also hunting tribes and powerful in war. In fact, they were the terror of their milder Algonkin neighbors. Person-ally, Iroquois Indians were finely built, strong, energetic, and active.

They spoke languages much alike and probably derived from one ancient language. This was believed by them to prove that the five tribes were related. Still they were at one time fre-quently at war with each other. This was before the white men came. Finally, a man named Hayenwatha was a chief among the Onondagas. He was wise, kind, and peaceable. There was at this same time another Onondaga chief named Atotarho, who was in character the opposite of Hayenwatha. He was a bold warrior and the dreaded foe of the Cayugas and Senecas, against whom he led war-parties; he was feared and dis-liked by his own people. When these two men were chiefs among the Onondagas, the Mohawks and the Oneidas were much harassed by their Algonkin neighbors, the Mohicans. Hayenwatha thought much over the sad condition of the Iroquois tribes. Constantly warring with their kindred in the west and troubled by outside foes

in the east, their future looked dark. He thought
of a plan of union which he believed would bring
peace and prosperity.

Most Indian tribes consisted of a few great
groups of persons, the members of which were
related to each other and lived together. Such
groups of related persons are called *gentes;* the sin-
gular of the word is *gens.* There were three gentes
among the Mohawks, three among the Oneidas,
and eight in each of the other three tribes. These
gentes usually bore the name of some animal;
thus the Oneida gentes were the wolf, bear, and
turtle. The people belonging to a gens were
called by the gens name. Thus an Oneida was
either a wolf, bear, or turtle. Every wolf was
related to every other wolf in his tribe; every
turtle to every other turtle; every bear to every
other bear.

Each tribe was ruled by a council which contained members elected from each gens. Each
gens had one or more councillors, according to
its size and importance. Each member of the
council watched with care to see that his gens
got all its rights and was not imposed upon by
others. Every tribe was independent of every
other tribe.

Hayenwatha's idea was to unite the tribes into
a strong confederacy. Separately the tribes were
weak, and a foe could do them much harm; united
they would be so strong that no one could trouble
them. He did not wish to destroy the tribes;

he wished each to remain independent in managing its own affairs; but he desired that together they should be one great power which would help all. Three times he called a council of his people, the Onondagas, to lay his plan before them; three times he failed because the dreaded Atotarho, who did not desire peace, opposed his scheme.

When he found he could not move his own people, Hayenwatha went to the Mohawks, where he found help; they agreed that such a union was needed. Next the Oneidas were interested. Two great chiefs, one Mohawk and one Oneida, then went to the Onondagas to urge these to join with them; again the plan failed because Atotarho opposed it. The two chiefs went further westward and had a council with the Cayugas, who were pleased with their plan. With a Cayuga chief to help them, they returned to the Onondagas. Another council was held, and finally the Onondagas were gained over by promising the chieftaincy of the confederacy to Atotarho. There was then no trouble in getting the consent of the Senecas. Two chiefs were appointed by them to talk over the plan with the others. Hayenwatha met the six chiefs at Onondaga Lake, where the whole plan was discussed and the new union was made.

It was at first "The Five Nations." At that time the Tuscaroras lived in the south. Later on, perhaps more than two hundred years later, they moved northward, and joined the confederacy,

making it " The Six Nations."   The Five Nations
formed one government under a great council.
This council consisted of fifty members — nine
Mohawks, nine Oneidas, fourteen Onondagas, ten
Cayugas, eight Senecas.   The names of the first
councillors were kept alive by their successors
always assuming them when they entered the
council.   The government did not interfere with
the rights of the different tribes.   It was always
ready to receive new tribes into itself.   Its purpose was said to be to abolish war and bring
general peace.   It did this by destroying tribes
that did not wish to unite with it.   At times the
Iroquois Confederacy really did receive other
tribes, such, for example, as the Tuteloes, Sapo-
nies, Tuscaroras, and fragments of the Eries and
Hurons.   They themselves always called the confederacy by a name meaning the "long house"
or the extended or drawn-out house.   The confederacy was thus likened "to a dwelling, which
was extended by additions made to the end, in
the manner in which their bark-built houses were
lengthened.   When the number of families in-
habiting these long dwellings was increased by
marriage or adoption, and a new hearth was
required, the end wall was removed, an addition
of the required size was made to the edifice, and
the closing wall was restored."

The confederacy became a great power, and is
often mentioned in history.   When the French
or English went to war, it was important for either

side to get the help of the Iroquois. In the council meetings of the tribes, and in the meetings of the great council of the confederacy, there were often important discussions. We have spoken of the warlike spirit of the Iroquois. A man who was a great warrior had great influence. So, however, had the man who was a great speaker. Oratory was much cultivated, and the man who, at a council, could move and sway his fellows, influencing them to war or peace, was an important person.

There were a number of the Iroquois orators whose names are remembered, but none is more famous than Red Jacket. We will give a passage from one of his speeches as an example of Indian oratory. The speech was made in 1805, at a council held at Buffalo. A missionary, named Cram, had come to preach to them, and invited a number of chiefs and important men to attend, that he might explain his business to them. After he had spoken, the old Seneca orator rose, and in his speech said the following words:

" Brother, listen to what we say. There was a time when our forefathers owned this great island. Their seats extended from the rising to the setting sun. The Great Spirit had made it for the use of Indians. He had created the buffalo, the deer, and other animals, for food. He made the bear and the beaver, and their skins served us for clothing. He had scattered them over the country, and taught us how to take them. He had caused the earth to produce corn for bread. All this he had done for his red children because he loved them. If we had any disputes about hunting grounds, they were generally settled without the shedding of much blood, but an evil day came upon us; your forefathers crossed the great water, and landed on this island. Their numbers were small; they found friends and not enemies; they told us they had fled from their country for fear of wicked men, and came here to enjoy their religion. They asked for a small seat; we took pity on them, granted their request, and they sat down among us; we gave them corn and meal; they gave us poison [whisky] in return. The white people had now found our country; tidings were carried back, and more came amongst us, yet we did not fear them; we took them to be friends; they called us brothers; we believed them, and gave them a larger seat. At length their numbers had greatly increased; they wanted more land; they wanted our country. Our eyes were opened, and our minds became uneasy. Wars took place; Indians were hired to fight against Indians, and many of our people were destroyed. They also brought strong liquors among us; it was strong and powerful, and has slain thousands.

" *Brother*, our seats were once large, and yours were very small; you have now become a great people, and we have scarcely a place left to spread our blankets; you have got our country, but are

not satisfied; you want to force your religion
upon us."

HORATIO HALE.—Explorer, linguist, ethnologist. One of
the earliest prominent American ethnologists. Among his important works is *The Iroquois Book of Rites.*

XVIII.

STORY OF MARY JEMISON.

YEARS ago, when I was a small boy, some one
pointed out to me the "old white woman's
spring," and told me a part of the story of
Mary Jemison.

In the year 1742 or 1743 an Irishman named
Thomas Jemison, with his wife and three children, left his own country for America, on a
ship called the *William and Mary*. On the
voyage a little girl was born into the family, to
whom they gave the name of Mary. She had
a light, clear skin, blue eyes, and yellow or
golden hair. After landing at Philadelphia, the
family soon moved to Marsh Creek (Pennsylvania), which was then in the far West and quite
in the Indian country. There Thomas Jemison
had a farm, built a comfortable house, and by
industry prospered. In the new home two
younger children were born, both boys.

In 1754 they moved to a new farm, where
they lived in a log house. Here they spent

the winter. Spring came, and every one was busy in the fields. It was the time of the French and Indian wars against the English. A number of attacks had been made upon settlers. One day Mary was sent to a neighbor's for a horse; she was to spend the night, returning in the morning. At that time some strangers were living at Mary's house — a man, his sister-in-law, and her three little children. Mary had secured the horse for which she had been sent, and had ridden home in the early morning. As she reached the house, the man took the horse and rode off to get some grain, taking with him his gun, in case he should see some game. Every one about the house was busy. Mary, years afterward, told the story of what then took place:

"Father was shaving an ax-helve at the side of the house; mother was making preparations for breakfast; my two oldest brothers were at work near the barn; and the little ones, with myself and the woman and her three children, were in the house. Breakfast was not yet ready, when we were alarmed by the discharge of a number of guns that seemed to be near. Mother and the woman before mentioned almost fainted at the report, and every one trembled with fear. On opening the door, the man and horse lay dead near the house, having just been shot by the Indians. I was afterward informed that the Indians discovered him at his own house with his gun, and pursued him to father's, where they shot him as I have related. They first secured my father, and then rushed into the house and without the least resistance made prisoners of my mother, brothers, and sister, the woman, her three children, and myself. . . . My two brothers Thomas and John, being at the barn, escaped."

The party which had seized them was composed of six Shawnee Indians and four Frenchmen. The first day was terrible. They were kept rapidly marching until night; they had no food or water during the whole day. One Indian went behind the party with a whip, with which he lashed the little ones to make them keep up with the party. At night there was no fire and they had no covering. They were afoot again before daylight, but as the sun rose, stopped and ate breakfast. The second night they camped near a dark and dreary swamp, and here they were given supper, but were too tired and sad to care much for food. After supper, an Indian stripped off Mary's shoes and stockings and began putting moccasins upon her. The same thing was done to the woman's little boy. Noticing this, Mary's mother believed the Indians intended to spare the two children. She said to the girl:

"My dear little Mary, I fear the time has arrived when we must be parted forever. Your life, I think, will be spared; but we shall probably be tomahawked here in this lonesome place, by the Indians. Alas! my dear, my heart bleeds at the thought of what awaits you; but if you leave us, remember your name, and the names of your father and mother. Be careful and not forget your English tongue. If you shall have an opportunity to get away from the Indians, don't try to escape; for if you do, they will find and destroy you. Don't forget, my little daughter, the prayers that I have learned you; say them often; be a good child, and God will bless you. May God bless you, my child, and make you comfortable and happy."

Just then an Indian took Mary and the little boy by the hand and led them away. As they parted, the mother called out to the child, who was crying bitterly, " Don't cry, Mary! Don't cry, my child! God will bless you! Farewell, farewell!"

The Indian took the children into the woods, where they lay down to sleep. The little boy begged Mary to try to escape, but she remembered her mother's warning. The next morning the other Indians and the Frenchmen rejoined them, but their white captives were not with them. During the night, in that dark and dismal swamp, Mary's father and mother, Robert, Matthew, and Betsey, the woman, and two of her children had been killed, scalped, and fearfully mangled. When they camped again, Mary saw with horror the Indians at work upon the scalps of her parents.

A fourth and fifth day the party journeyed on, and then, driven by bad weather, camped for three nights in one place. Finally the party came near Fort Du Quesne, where Pittsburg now stands. They had been joined by other Indians who had a young white man prisoner. When they reached this place, the Indians carefully combed the hair of the three prisoners, and painted their faces and hair with red as Indians do.

The next morning after they reached the fort, the little boy and young man were given to the French. Mary was given to two young Seneca women. By them she was taken to their town some distance down the Ohio River. Here they washed her and dressed her nicely in Indian clothing. They publicly adopted her in place of a brother who had just been killed. These women and their brothers were kind to Mary, treating her as their real sister, and she came to love them dearly. She was with them for three winters and two summers on the Ohio River, when, at their wish, she married a Delaware Indian named Shenanjie. He was a good husband, but died when they had been married but two or three years.

We will tell but one more incident in Mary's life. Not long after marrying Shenanjie, she moved with her sisters and their brothers to the Genesee Valley in New York. The wars were now over. Mary was a young widow with a little son. The King of England offered a bounty to

any one who would find white prisoners among
the Indians and bring them in to the forts to be
redeemed. A Dutchman named Van Sice, who
knew that Mary was a captive, determined to take
her to the fort and get his bounty. Mary learned
of his plan, but had no wish to leave the Indians.
She was afraid of the man. One day, when she
was working in the field alone, she saw him coming to seize her. He chased her, but she escaped
and hid herself for three days and nights. The
Indian council then decided that she could not
be taken back against her wish, and her fear of
Van Sice ceased.

But she had a more dangerous enemy. An old
chief of the tribe determined himself to return
her and get the bounty. He told one of Mary's
Indian brothers of his intention to take her to
Niagara to be redeemed. A quarrel took place
between the two men, and her brother declared
that he would kill her with his own hand before
he would allow the old man to carry her off
against her will. This threat he made known to
his own sister. She at once told Mary to flee
with her babe and hide in some weeds near the
house. She also told Mary that at night their
brother would return, informed of the old chief's
plans, and that if the sachem persisted in carrying
her off, he would surely kill her. The woman
told her, after it was dark to creep up to the
house, and if she found nothing near the door, to
come in, as all would be safe. Should she, how-

ever, find a cake there, she must flee. Poor Mary hid in the weeds with her baby boy; at night, when all was still, she crept up to the house; the little cake was there! Taking it, she fled to the spring now called, for that reason, "the white woman's spring." Her sister had suggested the place. That night the old chief came to the house to get Mary, and her brother sought her to kill her, but neither could find her. The old sachem gave up the hunt and set out for Niagara with his other prisoners. After he was gone, and the excitement was past, Mary's sister told her brother where Mary was hidden. He went there, and at finding her, greeted her kindly and brought her home.

JAMES E. SEAVER has written the story of Mary Jemison as she told it to him in her old age. The name of the book is *The Life of Mary Jemison: the White Woman of the Genesee.*

XIX.

THE CREEKS.

THE Creeks or Muskoki were one of the strongest tribes of the southern states. To them were related in language a number of important tribes — the Apalachi, Alibamu, Choctaw, Chicasaw, and others. Several of these tribes were united with the Creeks into a so-called confederacy. This union was not to be compared with that of the Iroquois or the Aztecs, but was a loose combination against foes.

The Creeks and their kindred tribes present a number of points of rather peculiar interest. In the olden time there were two kinds of Creek towns — white towns and red towns. The red towns were war towns, governed by warriors. The white or peace towns were governed by civil chiefs. It is said by some of the early writers that the white towns were "cities of refuge" to which those who were being pursued for some crime or unfortunate accident could flee. The red towns could be known as such as soon as a stranger entered the public square, as the posts of the "great house" were painted red.

Warriors were the most honored of men among the Creeks. Until a young man was successful in battle he was treated hardly different from a servant. The Creek boys had a pretty hard time. They were made to swim in the coldest weather; they were scratched with broken glass or fish teeth, from head to foot till the blood ran; these things were intended to toughen them to the endurance of pain. When the boy was fifteen to seventeen years old he was put through a test, after which he was no longer a boy, but a man. At the proper time he gathered an intoxicating plant. He ate the bitter root of it for a whole day, and drank a tea made of its leaves. When night came he ate a little pounded corn. He kept this up for four days. For four months he ate only pounded maize, which could only be cooked for him by a little girl. After that his food might be cooked by any one. For twelve months from the time of his first fast he ate no venison from young bucks, no turkeys nor hens, no peas nor salt; nor was he permitted to pick his ears or scratch his head with his fingers, but used a splinter of wood for the purpose. At the time of new moon he fasted four days, excepting that he ate a little pounded maize at night. When the last month of his twelve months' test came, he kept four days' fast, then burned some corncobs and rubbed his body with the ashes. At the end of that month, he took a heavy sweat and then plunged into cold water.

Men who wished to become great warriors selected some old conjurer to give them instruction. Four months were spent with him alone. The person desiring to learn fasted, ate bitter herbs, and suffered many hardships. After he had learned all the old conjurer could teach him, it was believed that he could disarm the enemy even at a distance, and if they were far away, could bring them near, so that he might capture them.

In the center of every large Creek town there was a public square. In this square there were three interesting things, — the great house, the council house, and the playground. The great house consisted of four one-story buildings, each about thirty feet long; they were arranged about a square upon which all faced. The side of these

which opened on the central square was entirely
open. . Each of the four houses was divided into
three rooms or compartments by low partitions of
clay. At the back of each compartment were
three platforms or seats, the lowest two feet high,
the second several feet higher, the third as much
higher than the second. These were covered
with cane matting, as if for carpeting. New mats
were put in each year, but the old ones were not
removed. Each of these four buildings was a
gathering-place for a different class of persons.
The one facing east was for the *miko* and people
of high rank; the northern building was for
warriors; the southern was for " the beloved
men "; and the eastern for the young people.
In the great house were kept the weapons, scalps,
and other trophies. Upon the supporting posts
and timbers were painted horned warriors, horned
alligators, horned rattlesnakes, etc. The central
court of the great house was dedicated ground,
and no woman might set foot in it. In the center
of it burned a perpetual fire of four logs.

The council house was at the northeast corner'
of the great house. It stood upon a circular
mound. It consisted of a great conical roof supported on an octagonal frame about twelve feet
high. It was from twenty-five to thirty feet in
diameter. Its walls were made of posts set upright and daubed with clay. A broad seat ran
around the house inside and was covered with
cane mats. A little hillock at the center formed

a fireplace. The fire kept burning upon this was fed with dry cane or finely split pine wood which was curiously arranged in a spiral line.

The council house was used as a gathering or meeting place, much as the great house, but it was chiefly for bad weather, especially for winter. Here, too, private meetings of importance were held at all times. Here young men prepared for war-parties, spending four days in drinking war-drink, and counseling with the conjurers. This council house was also the place for sweat baths. Stones were heated very hot; water was thrown upon them to give steam. Those desiring the bath danced around this fire and then plunged into cold water.

The playground was in the northwest corner of the public square; it was marked off by low embankments. In the center, on a low, circular mound, stood a four-sided pole, sometimes as much as forty feet high. A mark at the top served as a target for practice with the bow and arrow. The floor of this yard was beaten hard and level. The chief game played here was called Chunkey. It was played with neatly polished stone disks. These were set rolling along on the ground, and the players hurled darts or shafts at them to make the disk fall. (Compare with the wheel game of the Blackfeet.) Ball games and sometimes dances were also held upon this playground.

The great celebration of the Creeks was the

annual *busk*. They called it *puskita*, or fast. The
ceremony was chiefly held at the great house.
The time was determined by the condition of the
new corn and of a plant named cassine. The
ceremony lasted eight days and included many
details. Among them we can mention a few.
On the first day a spark of new fire was made
by rubbing two pieces of wood together. With
this a four days' fire was kindled; four logs of
wood were brought in and arranged so that one
end of each met one end of the others at the
middle, and the four formed a cross, the arms of
which pointed to the cardinal points; these were
fired with the spark of new fire. Bits of new fire,
at some time during the four days, were set outside where the women could take them to kindle
fresh fires on their home hearths.

At noon of the second day, the men took ashes
from the new fire and rubbed them over their
chin, neck, and body; they then ran and plunged
themselves into cold water. On their return, they
took the new corn of the year and rubbed it
between their hands and over their bodies. They
then feasted upon the new corn. On the last,
eighth day, of the busk, a medicinal liquid was
made from fourteen (or fifteen) different plants,
each of which had medicinal power; they were
steeped in water in two pots and were vigorously
stirred and beaten. The conjurers blew into the
liquid through a reed. The men all drank some
of this liquid and rubbed it over their joints.

They did other curious things during this day. When night came, all went to the river. "Old man's tobacco" was thrown into the stream by each person, and then all the men plunged into the river and picked up four stones from the bottom. With these they crossed themselves over the breast four times, each time throwing back one stone into the river.

Mr. Gatschet thinks that much good resulted from the busk. After it all quarrels were forgotten; crimes, except murder, were forgiven; old utensils were broken and new ones procured. Every one seemed to leave the past behind and begin anew.

ALBERT S. GATSCHET. — A Swiss, living in America : linguist, ethnologist. Connected with Bureàu of American Ethnology. Edited *A Migration Legend of the Creeks.*

XX.

THE PANI.

ALL the Plains Indians were rovers, buffalo hunters, and warriors; none of them were bolder or braver than the Pani. This tribal name is more frequently spelled Pawnee. The tribe belonged to the Caddoan family, which includes also the Caddoes and Wichitas and perhaps the Lipans and Tonkaways. The Pani were formerly numerous and occupied a large district in Nebraska. To-day they are few, and rapidly diminishing. In 1885 they numbered one thousand forty-five; in 1886, nine hundred ninety-eight; in 1888, nine hundred eighteen; in 1889, eight hundred sixty-nine. To-day they live upon a reservation in Oklahoma.

It is believed that the Pani came from the south, perhaps from some part of Mexico. They appear first to have gone to some portion of what is now Louisiana; later they migrated northward to the district where the whites first knew them. The name Pani means wolves, and the sign language name for the Pani consists of a representation of the ears of a wolf. Several reasons have been given for their bearing this name. Perhaps it was because they were as tireless and enduring as wolves; or it may be because they were skillful scouts, trailers, and hunters. They were in the habit of imitating wolves in order to get near camp for stealing horses. They threw wolfskins over themselves and crept cautiously near. Wolves were too common to attract much attention.

In the olden time the Pani hunted the buffalo on foot. Choosing a quiet day, so that the wind might not bear their scent to the herd, the hunters in a long line began to surround a little group of grazing buffalo. Some of the men were dressed in wolfskins, and crept along on all fours. When a circle had been formed around the animals, the hunters began to close in.

Presently one man shouted and shook his blanket
to scare the buffalo nearest him. The others did
the same, and in a short time the excited herd
was running blindly, turning now here and now
there, but always terrified by one or another of
the men in the now ever smaller circle. Finally
the animals were tired out with their running and
were shot and killed.

The way in which the Pani used to make
pottery vessels was simple and crude. The end
of a tree stump was smoothed for a mold. Clay
was mixed with burnt and pounded stone, to
give it a good texture, and was then molded over
this. The bowl when dry was lifted off and
baked in the fire. Sometimes, instead of thus
shaping bowls, they made a framework of twigs
which was lined with clay, and then burnt off,
leaving the lining as a baked vessel.

As long as they have been known to the
Whites, the Pani have been an agricultural
people. They raised corn, beans, pumpkins, and
squashes, which they said Tirawa himself, whom
they most worshiped, gave them. Corn was
sacred, and they had ceremonials connected with
it, and called it "mother." In cultivating their
fields they used hoes made of bone: these were
made by firmly fastening the shoulder-blade of a
buffalo to the end of a stick.

Two practices in which the Pani differed from
most Plains Indians remind us of some Mexican
tribes: they kept a sort of servants and sacrificed

human beings. Young men or boys who were
growing up often attached themselves to men of
importance. They lived in their houses and
received support from them: in return, they
drove in and saddled the horses, made the fire,
ran errands, and made themselves useful in all
possible ways.

The sacrifice of a human being to Tirawa —
and formerly to the morning star — was made
by one band of the Pani. When captives of
war were taken, all but one were adopted into
the tribe. That one was set apart for sacrifice.
He was selected for his beauty and strength. He
was kept by himself, fed on the best of everything, and treated most kindly.

Before the day fixed for the sacrifice, the people danced four nights and feasted four days.
Each woman, as she rose from eating, said to
the captive: " I have finished eating, and I hope
I may be blessed from Tirawa; that he- may
take pity on me; that when I put my seeds in
the ground they may grow, and that I may have
plenty of everything." You must remember that
this sacrifice was not a merely cruel act, but was
done as a gift to Tirawa, that he might give good
crops to the people. On the last night, bows
and arrows were prepared for every man and
boy in the village, even for the very little boys;
every woman had ready a lance or stick. By
daybreak the whole village was assembled at
the western end of the town, where two stout

posts with four cross-poles had been set up. To this framework the captive was tied. A fire was built below, and then the warrior who had captured the victim shot him through with an arrow. The body was then shot full of arrows by all the rest. These arrows were then removed, and the dead man's breast was opened and blood removed. All present touched the body, after which it was consumed by the fire, while the people prayed to Tirawa, and put their hands in the smoke of the fire, and hoped for success in war, and health, and good crops.

Almost all these facts about the Pani are from Mr. Grinnell's book. I shall quote from him now the story of Crooked Hand. He was a famous warrior. On one occasion the village had gone on a buffalo hunt, and no one was left behind except some sick, the old men, and a few boys, women, and children. Crooked Hand was among the sick. The Sioux planned to attack the town and destroy all who had been left behind. Six hundred of their warriors in all their display rode down openly to secure their expected easy victory. The town was in a panic. But when the news was brought to Crooked Hand lying sick in his lodge, he forgot his illness and, rising, gave forth his orders.

They were promptly obeyed. "The village must fight. Tottering old men, whose sinews were now too feeble to bend the bow, seized their long-disused arms and clambered on their

horses. Boys too young to hunt grasped the
weapons that they had as yet used only on
rabbits and ground squirrels, flung themselves
on their ponies, and rode with the old men.
Even squaws, taking what weapons they could,
— axes, hoes, mauls, pestles, — mounted horses
and marshaled themselves for battle. The force
for the defense numbered two hundred superan-
nuated old men, boys, and women. Among
them all were not, perhaps, ten active warriors,
and these had just risen from sick-beds to take
their place in the line of battle.

"As the Pawnees passed out of the village
into the plain, the Sioux saw for the first time
the force they had to meet. They laughed in
derision, calling out bitter jibes, and telling what
they would do when they had made the charge;
and, as Crooked Hand heard their laughter, he
smiled too, but not mirthfully.

"The battle began. It seemed like an un-
equal fight. Surely one charge would be enough
to overthrow this motley Pawnee throng, who
had ventured out to try to oppose the triumphal
march of the Sioux. But it was not ended so
quickly. The fight began about the middle of
the morning; and, to the amazement of the
Sioux, these old men with shrunken shanks and
piping voices, these children with their small,
white teeth and soft, round limbs, these women
clad in skirts and armed with hoes, held the
invaders where they were: they could make no

advance. A little later it became evident that the Pawnees were driving the Sioux back. Presently this backward movement became a retreat, the retreat a rout, the rout a wild panic. Then indeed the Pawnees made a great killing of their enemies. Crooked Hand, with his own hand, killed six of the Sioux, and had three horses shot under him. His wounds were many, but he laughed at them. He was content; he had saved the village."

From 1864 until 1876 the famous Pani scouts served our government faithfully. Those years were terrible on the Plains. White settlers were pressing westward. The Indians were desperate over the encroachments of the newcomers. Troubles constantly occurred between the pioneers and the Indians. During that sad and unsettled time, Lieutenant North and his Pani scouts served as a police to keep order and to punish violence.

XXI.

THE CHEROKEES.

THE old home of the Cherokees was in the beautiful mountain region of the South — in Georgia, North Carolina, and Tennessee, but especially in Georgia. They were Indians of great strength of character, and ready for im-

provement and progress. When Oglethorpe settled Georgia, the Cherokees were his friends and
allies. But after our government was established,
the tribe, which had been so friendly to the whites,
began to suffer from our encroachments. Treaties were made with them only to be broken
Little by little, the Indians were crowded back:
sacred promises made by our government were
not fulfilled.

Finally they refused to cede any more of their
land to the greedy white settlers, and demanded
that the United States protect them in their
rights. The quarrel was now one between the
United States and Georgia, and the central government found itself unable to keep its pledges.
So orders were given that the Cherokees should
be removed, even against their wish, to a new
home.

At this time the Cherokees were most happy
and prosperous. Their country was one of the
most lovely portions of our land. A writer says:
"The climate is delicious and healthy; the winters
are mild; the spring clothes the ground with the
richest scenery; flowers of exquisite beauty and va-
riegated hues meet and fascinate the eye in every
direction. In the plains and valleys the soil is
generally rich, producing Indian corn, wheat, oats,
indigo, and sweet and Irish potatoes. The natives carry on considerable trade with the adjoining states; some of them export cotton in boats
down the Tennessee to the Mississippi, and down

that river to New Orleans. Apple and peach orchards are quite common, and gardens are cultivated, and much attention paid to them. Butter and cheese are seen on Cherokee tables. There are many public roads in the nation, and houses of entertainment kept by natives. Numerous and flourishing villages are seen in every section of the country. Cotton and woolen cloths are manufactured; blankets of various dimensions, manufactured by Cherokee hands, are very common. Almost every family in the nation grows cotton for its own consumption. Industry and commercial enterprise are extending themselves in every part. Nearly all the merchants in the nation are native Cherokees. Agricultural pursuits engage the chief attention of the people. Different branches of mechanics are pursued. The population is rapidly increasing."

This was written in 1825. Only about ten years later, this happy, industrious, and prosperous people were removed by force from their so greatly loved home. Two years were allowed in which they must vacate lands that belonged to them, and which the United States had pledged should be always theirs. Few of them were gone when the two years had ended. In May, 1838, General Winfield Scott was sent with an army to remove them. He issued a proclamation which began as follows: —

"CHEROKEES, — The President of the United States has sent me with a powerful army to cause you, in accordance with the treaty of 1835, to join that part of your people who are already established on the other side of the Mississippi. Unhappily, the two years which were allowed for the purpose you have allowed to pass away without following, and without making any preparations to follow; and now, or by the time that this solemn address reaches your distant settlements, the emigration must be commenced in haste, but I hope without disorder. I have no power, by granting a further delay, to correct the error you have committed. The full moon of May is already on the wane, and before another shall have passed away, every Cherokee man, woman, and child in these states [1] must be in motion to join their brethren in the West."

And so this harmless, helpless people left for their long journey. Their only offense was that they owned land which the whites wanted. There are still old Indians who remember the " great removal." Most of them were little children then, but the sad leaving their beloved mountains and the sorrow and hardship of the long journey is remembered after sixty years.

A few years since, we visited the Eastern Cherokees. Perhaps two thousand of them now live in the mountains of North Carolina and Tennessee. Some of these are persons who never went to the Indian Territory, but hid themselves

[1] North Carolina, Georgia, Tennessee, Alabama.

in rocks and caves until the soldiers were gone; some ran away from the great company as it moved westward, trudging back a long and toilsome journey; some are the children and grandchildren of such refugees; some are persons who drifted back in later years to the hills and forests, the springs and brooks, which their fathers had known and loved. They are mostly poor, — unlike their relatives in the West, — but they are industrious and happy. Their log houses are scattered over the mountain slopes or perched upon the tops of ridges or clustered together in little villages in the pretty valleys. Their fields are fenced and well cultivated. They work them in companies of ten or twelve persons; such companies are formed to work the fields of each member in order. They dress like white people, and most of the old Indian life is gone.

Still there are some bits of it left. The women are basket-makers, and make baskets of wide splints of cane, plain or dyed black or red, which are interwoven to make striking patterns. Some old women weave artistically shaped baskets from slender splints of oak. Old Catolsta, more than ninety years old, still shapes pottery vessels and marks them with ornamental patterns which are cut upon a little paddle of wood, and stamped on the soft clay by beating it with the paddle. They still sometimes use the bow and arrow, though more in sport than in earnest, as most of them have white men's guns. The arrow race is still sometimes run. Several young men start out together, each with his bow and arrows. The arrows are shot out over the course; they run as fast as possible to where these fall and picking them up shoot them on at once. And so they go on over the whole course, each trying to get through first. Ball is largely a thing of the past, and great games are not common. Still there are rackets at many houses. One day we got a "scratcher" from old Hoyoneta, once a great medicine man for ball-players. This scratcher consisted of seven splinters of bone, sharpened at one end and inserted into a quill frame which held them firmly, separated from one another by about a

INDIAN BALL-PLAYER. (AFTER CATLIN.)

quarter of an inch or less. When a young man was about to play his first great game of ball, he went to Hoyoneta, or some other medicine man, to be scratched.

He had already fasted and otherwise prepared himself for the ordeal. The old man, after muttering charms and incantations, drew the scratcher four times the length of the young man's body, burying the points each time deeply in the flesh.

Each time the instrument made seven scratches. One set of these ran from the base of the left thumb, up the arm, diagonally across the chest, down the right leg to the right great toe; another, from the base of the right thumb to the left great toe; another, from the base of the left little finger, up the back of the arm, across the back, down the right leg to the base of the little toe; the other, from the base of the right little finger, to the left little toe. The young man then plunged, with all these bleeding gashes, into a cold running brook. He was then ready for the morrow's ball play, for, had he not been scratched twenty-eight times with the bones of swift running creatures, and been prayed over by a great medicine man?

Every one should know of Sequoyah or George Guess or Guest, as he was called in English. He was a Cherokee who loved to work at machinery and invent handy devices. He determined to invent a system of writing his language. He saw that the writing of the white men consisted in the use of characters to represent sounds. At first he thought of using one character for each word; this was not convenient because there are so many words. He finally concluded that there were eighty-six syllables in Cherokee, and he formed a series of eighty-six characters to represent them. Some of these characters were borrowed from the white man's alphabet; the rest were specially invented. It took some little time for the Cherokees to accept Sequoyah's great invention, but by 1827 it was in use throughout the nation.   Types were made, and soon books and papers were printed in the Cherokee language in Sequoyah's characters.   These are still

EXAMPLES OF SEQUOYAH'S CHARACTERS.

in use, and to-day in the Indian Territory, a newspaper is regularly printed by the Cherokee Nation, part of which is in English, part in the Cherokee character.   This newspaper is, by the way, supplied free to each family by the Cherokee government.

HELEN HUNT JACKSON. — Writer.   Her *nom de plume* was " H. H."   Wrote two books about Indians, *A Century of Dishonor* and *Ramona*.   Every American boy should read the former.

XXII.

GEORGE CATLIN AND HIS WORK.

A FAMOUS man in America fifty years ago was George Catlin.   He was born at Wyoming, Pennsylvania, in 1796, and lived to a good old age, dying in 1872. His father wished him to be a lawyer, and he studied for that profession and began its practice in Philadelphia. He was, however, fond of excitement and adventure, and found it hard to stick to his business. He was fond of painting, though he considered it only an amusement. While he was living in Philadelphia a party of Indians from the "Far West" spent some days in that city on their way to Washington. Catlin saw them, and was delighted with their fine forms and noble bearing. He determined to give up law practice and to devote his life to painting Indians, resolving to form a collection of portraits which should show, after they were gone, how they looked and how they lived.

He made his first journey to the Indian country for this purpose in 1832. For the next eight years he devoted himself to the work. He traveled many thousands of miles by canoe and horse, among tribes some of which were still quite wild. His life was full of excitement, difficulty, and danger. He made paintings everywhere: paintings of the scenery, of herds of buffalo, of hunting life, Indian games, celebrations of ceremonies, portraits — everything that would illustrate the life and the country of the Indian.

Among the tribes he visited were the Mandans, who lived along the Missouri River. Some of his best pictures were painted among them. He there witnessed the whole of their sun-dance ceremony, and painted four remarkable pictures

PORTRAIT OF GEORGE CATLIN.

of it. These represent the young men fasting in the dance lodge, the buffalo dance outside, the torture in the lodge, the almost equally horrible treatment of the dancers outside after the torture. Although a terrible picture, we have copied the painting showing the torture in the lodge (see next chapter) as an example of his work. Other pictures by him are the ball-player (see XXI.) and the chief in war dress (see I.).

Sometimes the Indians did not wish to be painted. They thought it would bring bad luck or shorten life. At one Sioux village the head chief was painted before any one knew it. When the picture was done, some of the headmen were invited to look at it. Then all the village wanted to see it, and it was hung outside the tent. This caused much excitement. Catlin says the medicine men "took a decided and noisy stand against the operations of my brush; haranguing the populace and predicting bad luck and premature death to all who submitted to so strange and unaccountable an operation! My business for some days was entirely at a stand for want of sitters; for the doctors were opposing me with all their force; and the women and children were crying with their hands over their mouths, making most pitiful and doleful laments."

At another town up the Missouri River, near the Yellowstone, there was a still greater excitement over one of Catlin's pictures. About six hundred Sioux families were gathered at a trading post from the several different sub-tribes of that great people. There had been some trouble over his painting, and the medicine men threatened that those who were painted would die or have great misfortune. An Uncpapa Sioux chief named Little Bear offered to be painted. He was a noble, fine-looking fellow, with a strong face which Catlin painted in profile. The picture was almost finished when a chief of a different band, a surly, bad-tempered man whom no one liked, came in. His name was Shonko, "The Dog." After looking at the picture some time, he at last said in an insolent way, "Little Bear is but half a man." The two men had some words, when finally The Dog said, "Ask the painter, he can tell you; he knows you are but half a man — he has painted but one half your face, and knows the other half is good for nothing." Again they bandied words back and forth, Little Bear plainly coming out ahead in the quarrel. The Dog hurried from the room in a great rage. Little Bear knew he was in danger; he hurried home, and loaded his gun to be prepared. He then threw himself on his face, praying to Wakanda for help and protection. His wife, fearing that he was bent on mischief, secretly removed the ball from his gun. At that moment the insolent voice of The Dog was heard. "If Little Bear is a whole man, let him come out and prove it; it is The Dog that speaks." Little Bear seized his gun and started to the door. His wife screamed

as she realized what she had done. It was too
late; the two men had fired, and Little Bear fell
mortally wounded in that side of his face which
had not been painted in the portrait. The Dog
fled.

The death of Little Bear called for vengeance.
Such an excitement arose that Catlin soon left,
going further up the river. The warriors of the
two bands organized war-parties, the one to protect, the other to destroy, The Dog. The Dog's
brother was killed. He was an excellent man,
and his death was greatly mourned. The Dog
kept out of reach. Councils were held. When
the matter was discussed, some things were said
which show the Indian ideas regarding portraits.
One man said:

" He [Catlin] was the death of Little Bear!
He made only one side of his face; he would not
make the other; the side he made was alive, the
other was dead, and Shonko shot it off." Another said: " Father, this medicine man [Catlin]
has done us much harm. You told our chiefs
and warriors they must be painted — you said
he was a good man and we believed you! you
thought so, my father, but you see what he has
done! he looks at our chiefs and our women and
then makes them alive! In this way he has
taken our chief away, and he can trouble their
spirits when they are dead! they will be un-
happy." On his return voyage Catlin had to be
cautious, and avoided the Uncpapa encampment.

Some months later The Dog was overtaken and killed.

Catlin's pictures varied much in quality. Some were fine; others were poor. Often he made the outlines and striking features wonderfully well.

Catlin was among the Mandans in 1832. Thirty-three years later Washington Matthews was in the Upper Missouri country. He had with him a copy of Catlin's book with line pictures of more than three hundred of his paintings. The Indians had completely forgotten Catlin and his visit, but were much interested in his pictures.

The news soon spread that the white man had a book containing the "faces of their fathers." Many went up to Fort Stevenson to see them. They recognized many of the portraits and expressed great emotion. That is, the women did, weeping readily on seeing them. The men seemed little moved. One day there came from the Mandan town, sixteen miles away, the chief, Rushing Eagle, son of Four Bears, who had been a favorite of Catlin's. Catlin painted him several times (see opposite page 1). When the son saw his father's picture, though he gazed at it long and steadily, he showed no emotion. Dr. Matthews was called away on some errand, and told the chief that he would be away some time and left him alone with the book. He was obliged, however, to return for something, and was surprised to find Rushing Eagle weeping and earnestly addressing his father's portrait.

Catlin not only painted hundreds of pictures among many tribes; he also secured many fine Indian objects — dress, weapons, scalps, objects used in games, painted blankets, etc. With his pictures and curiosities, which had cost him so much time, labor, and danger, he traveled through the United States.

He exhibited in Boston, New York, Philadelphia, Washington, and many less important cities, and everywhere attracted crowds. He went to Europe and exhibited in France, Belgium, and England. Every one spoke of him. He was the guest of kings and prominent men everywhere. Louis Philippe, King of France, was so much interested in his work that he proposed to buy the pictures and curiosities for the French nation. But just then came the Revolution which dethroned him, and the sale fell through. Many of Catlin's pictures and some of his curiosities are still in existence, and the greater part of these are in the United States National Museum at Washington.

WASHINGTON MATTHEWS. — Physician, ethnologist. Author of important works regarding the Hidatsa and Navajo Indians. Wrote *The Catlin Collection of Indian Paintings.*

XXIII.

THE SUN DANCE.

THE Sioux or Dakota Indians are one of the largest tribes left. They live at present chiefly in the states of North and South Dakota. There are a number of divisions or sub-tribes of them — the Santee, Sisseton, Wahpeton, Yankton, Yanktonnais, and Teton Sioux. The Tetons in turn are divided into several bands each with its own name. These are all Sioux proper, but there are many other tribes that speak languages that are related to the Sioux. Among these Siouan — but not Sioux — tribes are the Winnebagoes, Mandans, Poncas, Assinaboines, Omahas, and Otoes.

The Sioux are tall, finely built Indians, with large features and heavy, massive faces. They are a good type of the Plains Indians who until lately lived by hunting buffalo. There are now nearly thirty thousand true Sioux and about ten thousand Siouans of related tribes.

Among all peoples of the Siouan family it is probable that the terrible sun dance was practiced. It differed somewhat from tribe to tribe. It was seen and described by a number of whites, but to-day it has been forbidden by the United States government, and it is some years since it last took place.

The sun dance was made to please Wakantanka, the sun.   If there were a famine or disease,
or if one wished success in war, or to have a good
crop, a young man would say, " I will pray to
Wakantanka early in the summer."   The man at
once began to prepare for the event.   He took
sweat baths, drank herb teas, and gave feasts to
his friends, where herb teas were used.   He had
to be careful of what things he touched; used a
new knife, which no one else might use; must
not touch any unclean thing.   He could not go
in swimming.   He and his friends gathered together all the property they could, that he might
give many gifts at the time of the dance.

At his house every one had to treat him kindly
and not vex him.   An *umane* was made near the
back of the tent.   This was a space dug down to
the lower soil.   Red paint was strewn over it, and
no one might set foot upon it.   Any of those who
were to take part in the dance, after he had
smoked would carefully empty the ashes from his
pipe upon this spot.   The spot represented life
as belonging to the earth.

Invitations to neighboring tribes were sent
early, and long before the dance parties began
to arrive.   Some of these would spend several
weeks about the village.   At first they pitched
their camps wherever it best suited them.   A
little before the dance orders were given, and all
the visitors camped in one large camp circle, each
tribe occupying a special place.   The space within

this circle was carefully leveled and prepared. A special building was erected in the center of this circle in which the young men made their preparations. In it were buffalo skulls, — one for each dancer, — a new knife and ax, and couches of sage for the dancers to lie upon.

A sacred tree was next secured and set up. This was an important matter. Men of consequence were first sent out to select it. When they had found one they announced it in the village, and a great crowd rode out on horseback to the spot. Many strange things were done in getting it, but at last it was cut down. A bundle of wood, a blanket, a buffalo robe, and two pieces of buffalo skin — one cut to the shape of a man, the other to that of a buffalo — were fastened in the tree. It was then carried in triumph back to the camp and set up.

A dance house was built around this tree. It was like a great ring in shape, and the space between it and the tree was not roofed. The dance house was built of poles and leaves. In it all the more important parts of the ceremony were performed. After the tree was set up and the dance house built, all the town was in excitement; men, dressed in all their finery, went dashing on horseback around the camp circle, shooting their pistols and making a great noise. The old men shot at the objects hung in the sacred tree. At evening the young men and women rode around, singing.

During all this time the young men had been preparing for the dance: They were especially dressed, they had sung, drummed, and smoked. When the evening came that has been described, the dance really began. The young men danced from the lodge, where they had been making preparation, to the dance lodge.

The leader carried a buffalo skull painted red. All cried as they went. On entering the dancing house they saluted the four cardinal points and seated themselves at the back of the lodge, singing. A spot, shaped like a crescent, was then cut in the ground, and the dancers placed in it the buffalo skulls they carried. Shortly afterward began the tortures, which have made this dance so famous. They were intended to test the bravery of the young men and to please the sun. Sometimes a man stood between four posts arranged in the form of a square. His flesh was cut in two places in the back, and thongs were passed through and tied to the post in front. Another had a buffalo skull hung to the thong passed through his back, and danced until the weight of the skull tore out the thong. From a pole hung eight thongs; one man took two of these and passed them through his cuts and fastened them; he then hung back and looked upward at the sun. Other men, who did not take part in the dance itself, sat near the sun pole, and with new knives cut bits of flesh from their shoulders and held them up to the sun pole. Some-

times a man took his horse with him into the
dancing lodge. His chest was pierced in two
places and thongs from the pole were inserted;
he was then tied to his horse, and the animal
was whipped up. The thongs were thus suddenly jerked and the flesh torn.

These are only a few of the dreadful things

TORTURES OF THE MANDAN SUN DANCE. (AFTER CATLIN.)

that have been told of sun-dance tortures. They
are taken from a description given by an Indian
named George Bushotter. He not only described
the dance, but drew a curious lot of rude pictures
showing it.

Years before, George Catlin saw the sun dance
of the Mandans, and left four terrible pictures of

it. The celebration at that time among the Mandans exceeded in the horror of its tortures that which we have described.

While these tortures were going on in the dancing lodge, all sorts of things were being done outside. The old women danced. Songs were sung in honor of the young men. Children were gathered together and their ears were pierced. Presents were given away. A double fence of poles connected the house of preparation and the dance house, and upon it objects of all kinds were hung. These were free gifts to any one who chose to take them.

From the time the sacred tree was set up until the dance was over, the young men taking part fasted and took no drink. While they suffered, and as they gazed at the sun or lifted up their hands toward it, they continually prayed, saying, "Please pity me; bring to pass the things I desire." When all was over, the young men were taken home, and each was given four sips of water and a bit of food. A little later they might eat all they liked. Then they went into the sweat lodge. They were now through, and ever after might boast of having danced to Wakantanka.

J. Owen Dorsey. — Missionary, ethnologist. Was connected with the Bureau of Ethnology. Wrote many papers, one of which is *Siouan Cults*.

XXIV.

THE PUEBLOS.

THE most interesting Indians of the Southwest are the Pueblos, so called from their habit of living in towns. The word Pueblo is Spanish, and means a village or town. More than three hundred years ago the Spaniards, exploring northward from Mexico, found these clusters of industrious Indians living in their quaint towns. They conquered them and brought them missionaries. They taught them their beautiful language, and even to-day Spanish is spoken in all the pueblos in addition to the native Indian tongue. When the Spaniards entered New Mexico there were more than one hundred pueblos; to-day there are about twenty. Most of these are in New Mexico, but seven, the Moki towns, are in Arizona.

The home of the Pueblos is a wonderful land. It is a country of desert, of flat-topped *mesas*, of sharp-pinnacled crests, of broad valleys, and deep and narrow cañons. It is a land where the sky is almost always blue, and where the air is clear. There are but few streams, and every spring is precious. The people always built near water, and selected some spot in a valley where there was room for the corn-fields.

The largest of the present pueblos is Zuñi, in New Mexico. Some years ago a white man,

Frank Cushing, went to Zuñi and lived for a long time there to learn about the life and customs of the Pueblo Indians. They were kind to him, at first taking him into their own houses, and later allowing him a little house by himself. Since Mr. Cushing went to live at Zuñi, a number of other persons have lived at other pueblos, so that we know a good deal about them now.

VIEW OF PUEBLO: TAOS, N. M. (FROM PHOTOGRAPH.)

In former times a pueblo consisted of one great house, or, at most, of a few great houses, each the home of a large number of people. Taos, in northern New Mexico, is, perhaps, as old-fashioned as any of the pueblos now occupied. Even to-day it consists almost entirely of two large houses, one on each side of the little Taos River. The houses are so built that the flat roofs of the different stories form a set of steps as one looks at them from in front. In a three-story building the lower floor would have three sets of rooms, one in front of another. The roof of the front line of rooms would form a flat platform in front of the front rooms of the second story, which consisted only of two lines of rooms. The roof of the front line of these, in turn, was a platform in front of the single line of third-story rooms. Formerly there were no doors in the lower rooms, but ladders were placed against the wall, and persons climbed up on the roof; then through a hole in the roof, by means of another ladder they climbed down into the room. By ladders from the roof of the first floor they climbed to the top of the second story; there were doors in the rooms of the second and third stories. Nowadays there are usually doors into the lower rooms, but they still use ladders for getting into the upper stories.

The people are fond of sitting on the house-tops as they work. There they spin, shell corn, cut and dry squashes, shape pottery vessels, etc. There they gather in crowds when there are dances in the pueblo, and when there are foot races or pony races.

The walls of these houses are built of stone covered over with adobe mud, or of sundried adobe bricks. They did not formerly have what we would call windows, but there were small openings in the walls for air, or for peepholes. In the pueblos of to-day we find true sashes with glass in a few of the houses. There are also some rather old rooms that have windows made of "isinglass" or gypsum, a mineral found in the mountains, which can be split into thin sheets, which are transparent. The chimneys in these houses are made of broken water-jars laid up, one on another, and the joints plastered with mud.

PUEBLO POTTERY. (FROM ORIGINALS IN PEABODY MUSEUM.)

The Pueblo Indians are industrious. The men have to attend to their fields, their orchards of peaches and apricots, and their flocks and herds. The women tend the gardens, make pottery and baskets, and prepare the food. Men are also weavers of blankets and belts. The produce of the fields is chiefly corn, but some wheat is also raised. Considerable crops are made of water-melons, muskmelons, squashes, and gourds. The most important domestic animals are ponies, the little donkeys called *burros*, and goats. Near the pueblos are always several enclosures built of poles set in the ground, called *corrals*. These are for the animals, and one kind only is usually kept in one corral. The Indian boys have great fun at evening when the burros are brought home from pasture and put into the corral. They go in among them and play until dark

ESTUFA AT COCHITI, N. M. (FROM PHOTOGRAPH.)

with the patient little beasts. They climb up on to them and ride, push, pull, and tease them. Early the next morning the whole herd is taken out to pasture by two or three boys, whose work it is to stay with them all day.

A visitor to a pueblo would be sure to notice the *estufas*. These differ with the pueblo, but the characteristic Rio Grande pueblo type is a large, round, single-roomed, flat-topped building.

They are smoothly coated outside with adobe clay. A flight of steps leads to the roof, and a long ladder projecting through a hole in the roof leads down to the inside. The floor of the estufa is considerably lower than the ground outside. Years ago, before the Spanish priests taught the Indians our ideas of family life, all the men and large boys slept in the estufa at night, while the women and little children slept in the big houses. Nowadays the estufas are somewhat mysterious places where the dancers practice for the great dances, and where, on the day of celebration, they dress and ornament for the event.

At the pueblos are many little round-topped buildings of clay and stone. They have a small opening or door at the bottom. They are the ovens for baking bread. The women build a fine fire of dry brush inside the oven until it is heated thoroughly. The ashes and coals are then raked out, and the loaves of bread, shaped like large rolls, are put inside on the floor, and a sheepskin is hung at the door. In about an hour the bread is removed, well baked and piping hot. Some years ago a lady visiting Taos wrote a description of that pueblo. She mentioned these clay ovens, and said, "When not in use for baking bread, they make nice dog kennels." We have never seen any except such as had the doorway carefully filled up with stones when they were not in use for baking.

The bread baked in these ovens is made of wheat flour. Another kind, called paper-bread, is made of corn. The chief work of the Pueblo woman is grinding corn meal. The grinding is done upon a stone set slantingly on the ground. This stone is called a *metaté*. The woman kneels in front of it and holds a rubbing stone in her hands. Throwing a handful of grains of corn upon the metaté, she rubs it to meal with the rubbing stone. It is hard work, and the woman's body moves up and down, up and down, as she grinds. Usually she sings in time to her movements. Sometimes three or four grindstones are set side by side, separated from each other by boards. Several women grind together, each at one of the stones. The first grinds the corn to a coarse meal; she then passes it to the next, who grinds it finer, and then passes it along to be made still finer.

In making paper-bread fine corn meal is mixed with water into a dough or batter. A fire is then built under a flat stone with a smooth top. When this is hot, the woman spreads a thin sheet of dough upon it with her hand; in a moment this is turned, and then the sheet, which is almost as thin as paper, is folded or rolled up and is ready to eat. The color of paper-bread varies, but commonly it is a dull bluish-green and tastes sweet and good.

For threshing wheat the Pueblos prepare a clean, round spot of ground, perhaps twenty feet across. It is smooth, with a hard, well-trodden floor of clay. It is surrounded with a circle of poles stuck in the ground, to which ropes are fastened in order to make an enclosure.

The grain, cut in the fields, is brought in and heaped up on the clay floor. Ponies are driven into the enclosure, and a boy with a whip keeps them running around. They tread the grain loose from the chaff or husk. In the afternoon, when the wind has risen, men with wooden shovels and pitchforks throw the grain and chaff into the air. The wheat, being heavy, falls, while the chaff is blown away. When the grain has thus been nearly cleaned, the women come with great bowl-shaped baskets. Spreading a blanket or skin robe on the ground, a woman takes a basketful of the grain, holds it up above her head, and gently shakes it from side to side, pouring out a little stream of the grain all the time. As this falls, the wind blows out the last of the chaff and dirt, and the grain is left clean, ready for use.

XXV.

THE SNAKE DANCE.

IN northeastern Arizona, in a region of unusual wildness, even for the Southwest, lies the Moki Reservation. There are seven Moki pueb-

los built on the crests of the mesas. All are
built of stone. The two largest are Walpi and
Oraibe. Six of these towns speak a language
related to that of the Shoshones; the seventh,
Hano, is a settlement of strangers from the east,
who speak the language of Taos on the Rio
Grande. The Moki pueblos are, in some ways,
particularly old-fashioned. Here the women do
their hair up curiously: it is parted in the middle, and neatly smoothed out at the sides; behind it is done up in two queer, rounded masses,
like horns. Formerly, perhaps, the women at
some other pueblos wore their hair in this same
way. In these Moki towns they weave the dark
blue or black woolen *mantas*, or dresses, which
are worn by women in all the other pueblos.

In most respects the life of the Moki is like
that of other Pueblo Indians. There is, however, among them a great religious ceremony,
which is famous, and is perhaps the wildest and
weirdest of all Indian rituals. This is the *Snake
Dance*. It is held at any one town only once
in two years, but it occurs at some town or other
every year. Thus it is held at Walpi in the
odd years — 1899, 1901; it is held at Oraibe,
the even years — 1900, 1902, etc. It is cele-
brated about the middle of August, and always
attracts a crowd of Indian and white visitors.

The whole ceremony, of which the snake
dance is a part, requires nine days or more, for
its celebration. Most of the things are done in

the *kiva*, or *estufa*, secretly. Dr. Fewkes has given a full account of these, some of which are very curious. During the earlier days runners are sent out to place prayer sticks at the springs and sacred places. The first days they are sent out the messengers go to the more distant shrines, but each day take in places nearer and nearer home. During the fifth, sixth, seventh, and eighth days snake hunts take place ; the hunter priests go out to capture living snakes. The first day they go to the north, the second to the west, the third to the south, the fourth to the east. All kinds of snakes are taken, though perhaps the rattlesnakes are most prized. Few white men have ever seen the snake hunt. One who has seen it writes:

"In a short time a low call came from a man who was thrusting his stick into a dense clump of greasewood, and as the hunters gathered, there was found to be a large rattlesnake, lying in the heart of the thicket. Without hesitation they at once proceeded to cut away the bushes with their hoes, and strangely enough, although the snake lay in coil and watching them, it made no rattling or other display of anger. One of the twigs fell upon it, and the man nearest stooped down and deliberately lifted the branch away. Each one then sprinkled a pinch of meal upon the snake, and the man who had found it bent over and tapped it lightly with the feathers of his snake whip, and then it straightened out to make off, but just as it relaxed from coil, the hunter, using his right hand, in which he held his snake whip, instantly seized it a few inches back of the head. Holding it out, he gave it a quick shake, and then proceeded to fold it up and put it in one of the small bags carried for this purpose, showing no more concern in its handling than if it had been a ribbon." All these snakes are cared for, being put into jars or vessels in the kiva.

We can speak of few things in the kiva. The altars of colored sands, the dances, the songs, the sacred vessels, and other objects used, the dramatic representation of passages from their legends, are all curious. We have not time to speak of them. On the eighth day, the priests of the antelope society dance, sing the sixteen songs, and perform a drama, all in the kiva. At last the ninth day arrives.

The plaza, or square, in the middle of the town has been prepared. In it is the *kisi*, built of green boughs, intended as a shelter for the snakes. In front of it is a board in which is a hole, called the *sipapu*. This hole is supposed to lead down into the lower world, where people used to live. Early in the morning there was a race between boys and girls. They went first to the fields, and then raced in, each bringing a load of melon vines, corn plants, or other vegetable life. These they placed in the plaza.

At noon the snakes are washed in the kiva. A great bowl is brought in and carefully set down,

Into it liquid is poured from the north, west, south, and east. The snakes, which have been kept in jars at the corners of the room, are taken and handed to certain priests near the washbowl. All those in the kiva begin to shake their rattles and to sing in a low, humming voice. The priests holding the snakes begin to beat time with them up and down above the liquid. The song increases, becoming "louder and wilder, until it bursts forth into a fierce, blood-curdling yell, or war-cry. At this moment the heads of the snakes were thrust several times into the liquid, so that even parts of their bodies were submerged, and were then drawn out, not having left the hands of the priests, and forcibly thrown across the room upon the sand mosaic. . . . As they fell on the sand picture, three snake priests stood in readiness, and while the reptiles squirmed about, or coiled for defense, these men, with their snake whips, brushed them back and forth in the sand of the altar. . . . The low, weird song continued while other rattlesnakes were taken in the hands of the priests, and as the song rose again to the wild war-cry, these snakes were also plunged into the liquid and thrown upon the writhing mass, which now occupied the place of the altar. . . . Every snake in the collection was thus washed."

Late in the afternoon, near sunset, the antelope priests in all their finery and paint appear in a procession and circle four times around the plaza, dancing as they go and thumping heavily

upon the board in front of the kisi as they pass
over it. Then they draw up in line before the
kisi. Then the snake priests come out of their
kiva, with bodies painted red and their chins black,
with white lines. They wear dark red kilts and
moccasins. They dance four times around the
plaza, but with more energy and wildness than
the antelope priests had done. They then draw
up in a line opposite the antelope priests and go
through with strange singing and movements.

Suddenly the party of snake priests divides
into bands of three persons. These little bands
approach the kisi, where the snakes have been
placed. One of the men kneels, and when
he rises holds a snake in his hand. This he
places squirming in his mouth, holding it at
about the middle of its body. One of his companions throws an arm about the neck of the
snake carrier; in his other hand he holds a
feather wand or brush, with which he brushes at
the snake as if to attract his attention. The
third man of the band follows the other two. In
this way they go with the wriggling snake. Four
times these bands of three go around the plaza,
when the snakes are dropped. The followers
catch them up at once. When all the snakes
have been danced with and are gathered into the
arms of the followers, an old priest advances into
the center of the plaza and makes a ring of sacred
meal. Those holding the snakes run up and
throw them into one squirming, writhing mass

within this ring. All the priests then rush in, seize what snakes they can, and dart with them, down the trail, out into the open country, where they release the snakes to go where they please. Meantime, the antelope priests close the public ceremony by marching gravely four times round the plaza.

This ceremony is a prayer for rain. It also celebrates in a dramatic form the story of how the great snake and antelope societies began. The snakes gathered in the fields hear the prayers of the people, and when they are loosed carry them to the gods.

JESSE WALTER FEWKES. — Naturalist, ethnologist. Now with the Bureau of Ethnology, Washington, D.C. Has written a number of papers about the snake dance.

JOHN G. BOURKE. — Soldier, ethnologist. Was the first American ethnologist to describe the *Snake Dance of the Moki.*

XXVI.

CLIFF DWELLINGS AND RUINS OF THE SOUTHWEST.

THROUGH a large area in Colorado, New Mexico, Arizona, and Utah, also in parts of northern Mexico, there are found several kinds of ancient ruins. At some places they are pretty well preserved, and walls still stand to a considerable height. At others they are mere heaps of stone blocks or crumbling adobe bricks. The three best defined types of buildings found in these ruins are old pueblos, cliff ruins, and cave houses.

Zuñi is the largest inhabited pueblo. Not far from it lies Old Zuñi; and under the ruins of Old Zuñi lie the ruins of a yet older pueblo. Such ruins of old pueblos number hundreds in the Southwest. Sometimes the old walls were built of stone, carefully laid, and with the cracks neatly chinked with splinters of stone; sometimes the stones of the walls were laid in adobe cement; sometimes the walls were constructed of great adobe bricks. These old pueblos were in style and character like those now inhabited. They were often three or four stories high and terraced from in front back. Sometimes they were elliptical or rounded in general form, but more commonly they were built around the three sides of a central court, upon which the buildings faced. Some of these old pueblos were larger than any now occupied, and many of them were better built.

The cliff dwellings were built on ledges of rock along the sides of cliffs. Many of the streams of the Southwest flow through deep and narrow gorges cut in the solid rock. Such gorges are there called cañons. Among the famous cliff dwellings are those in the cañon of the Chelley River, and those in Mancos Cañon. Here are houses perched up on ledges or stowed away in natural caverns. Some of them are hundreds of feet above the stream, and have a perpendicular rock wall for one hundred feet below them. These

houses are carefully built with stone laid
cement.   Besides houses of many rooms, :
of two or more stories, there are circular tow
Plainly, the people who built these houses di
to secure themselves from attack.   Their gard
and fields must have been far below in the val
   The cave houses were usually dug out in
rocks by human beings.   They were cut in

CLIFF RUINS AT MANCOS CAÑON. (AFTER PHOTOGRAPH.)

soft rock with picks or axes of stone.   Some
these dwellings were cut out as simple open ca
In such, there were walls erected at the fr
The cave might be so cut that the rock face
mained for the front wall of the house; a l
was first cut for a doorway, and then the room
rooms would be dug out from it behind the
wall.
   Some persons believe these three kinds

houses were built by three distinct peoples or tribes. This is not likely, for sometimes two or all three kinds are found together, so related as to show that all were occupied at one time by the people of one village.

About twenty or twenty-five miles up the Rio Grande from the pueblo of Cochiti, New Mexico, is a brook called *El Rito de los Frijoles*, which means "the brook of the beans." It runs in a fine gorge with rock banks; large pine trees grow in the valley and cap the summits of the chasm. In one of the side cliffs are hundreds of holes, the remains of old dug cave rooms and houses. In most of them the rock cliff face itself forms the front wall of the house. We entered one single-roomed house that looked almost as if it had been used yesterday.

We crept in through a little doorway about a dozen feet up in the cliff and found ourselves in a small room about fifteen feet square. We could see the marks on the roof and the upper part of the walls, where stone picks had been used in cutting out the house. The floor was neatly smoothed, and covered with hard clay. The lower part of the wall was finished smooth with clay, washed over with a thin coat of fine cream-colored clay. The roof was black with the smoke of ancient fires; a little smoke-hole pierced the forward wall, near and above, but at one side of, the door. There were niches cut out in the wall, where little treasures used to be kept. Ends of poles set in the rock seemed to be pegs upon which objects were hung; their unevenly cut ends showed the marks of stone axes. In the floor we found a line of loops to which the bottom pole of the old blanket-weaving loom must have been fastened.

But these cave houses are not the only ruins at El Rito. Along certain parts of the cliff are remains of ancient buildings of the true pueblo type, which had been built against the base of the cliff. They are often placed in such a way with reference to cave rooms in the cliff as to show that both were parts of one great building. Thus, on the ground floor there might be two pueblo rooms in front of a cave room, on the second floor there might be one pueblo room in front of one cave room, and on the third floor there might be only cave rooms. Following up the cañon a little way from this mass of ruins, passing other cave houses, and heaped-up rubbish of old pueblo walls, on the way, we see, perhaps a hundred feet up the cliff, a great natural cavern. Climbing to it, we find as genuine cliff houses constructed therein as those of Mancos Cañon itself. It is certain that at El Rito the people built at one time the three kinds of houses, — the pueblo, the cliff house, the cave house.

At El Rito we find what is common near these ruins in many places, — great numbers of pictures cut in the rock wall. These pictures are some-times painted as well as cut in, and often repre-

sent the sun, the moon, human beings, and ani·
mals.

Many relics are found at these ruins. The
old *metatés* and rubbing stones for grinding
meal are common. Axes, adzes, and picks of
stone are not rare, and once in a ν ,ile a speci-
men is found with the old handle still attached.
These stone tools have a groove around the
blade. A flexible branch was bent around this
and tied, thus forming the handle. Many round
pebbles are found which are much battered;
these were hammers. Pieces of sandstone are
found with straight grooves worn across them;
they were used to straighten and smooth arrows
on. Arrow heads and spear heads made of chert,
jasper, chalcedony, and obsidian, are common.
Sometimes yarns of different colors, bits of cloth,
and objects made of hair are found. Sandals
neatly woven of yucca fiber are common.

In many of these old caves dried bodies have
been found. They are usually called " mummies,"
but wrongly so. Sometimes sandals are found
still upon their feet, and not rarely the blankets
made of feather cloth, in which they were
wrapped, are preserved. This was made by
fastening feathers into a rather open-work cloth
of cords.

The art of all arts, however, among the people
who built these ancient houses is the one in
which modern Pueblos excel, — pottery. Thou·
sands of whole vessels have been taken from

these ruins.   There are many forms, — great water-jars, flasks, cups, bowls, ladles, — and, in ware and decoration, they are much better than those made by modern Pueblos.   The ware is generally thinner, better baked, firmer, and gives a better ring when struck.   The decorations are usually good geometrical designs.

The ancient builders were, in culture, mode of life, and architecture, much like the modern Pueblos.   It is probable that some of them were the ancestors of the Pueblo Indians.   The Mokis claim that some of the ruins of the McElmo Cañon were the old homes of their people; and the inhabitants of Cochiti assert that it was their forefathers who lived at *El Rito de los Frijoles.*   We cannot say of every ruined building who built it, but certainly the builders were Indians very like the Pueblos.

ADOLF F. BANDELIER. — Historian, archæologist; made an extended study of the ruins of New Mexico, Arizona, and northern Mexico.

XXVII.

TRIBES OF THE NORTHWEST COAST.

A LONG and narrow strip of land stretches from Vancouver Island northward to Alaska.   It is bounded on the east by the great mountains, on the west by the Pacific Ocean.   Its coast line is irregular; narrow fiords run far into the land. The climate is generally temperate, but there is much rain. Dense forests of pine, cedar, hemlock, and maple cover the mountain slopes. Many kinds of berries grow there abundantly, supplying food for man. In the mountain forests are deer, elk, caribou; both black and grizzly bears are found; wolves are not uncommon. In the remoter mountains are mountain sheep and mountain goats. Beaver and otter swim in the fresh waters, while the seal, fur seal, sea-lion, and whale are found in the sea. In the waters are also many fish, such as halibut, cod, salmon, herring, and oolachen; shell-fish are abundant.

In this interesting land are many different tribes of Indians, speaking languages which in some cases are very unlike. Among the more important tribes or group of tribes, are the Tlingit, Haida, Tshimpshian, and Kwakiutl. While all these tribes are plainly Indians, there are many persons among them who are light-skinned and brown-haired. The hair is also at times quite wavy. The forms are good and the faces pleasing.

But these Indians are not always satisfied with the forms and faces nature gives them. They have various fashions which change their appearance. Among these is changing the shape of the head. Formerly the Chinooks, living near the Columbia River, changed the shape of all the baby boys' heads. The bones of the head in a little baby are soft and can be pressed out of shape. As the child grows older, the bones become harder and cannot be easily altered. The Chinooks made the little head wedge-shaped in a side view. This was done by a board, which was hinged to the cradle-board, and brought down upon the little boy's forehead. It forced the head to broaden in front and the forehead to slant sharply. After the pressure had been kept on for some months, the shape of the head was fixed for life. From the strange shape of their heads thus produced, the Chinooks were often called "Flat-

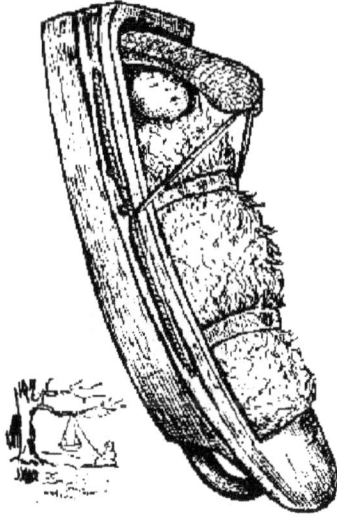

CHINOOK BABY IN CRADLE. (FROM MASON.)

heads." On Vancouver Island the head of the Koskimo baby girl was forced by circular bandages wrapped around it to grow long and cylindrical.

Another fashion among the women of some tribes was the piercing of the lower lip for the wearing of a plug as an ornament. Thus, when a little girl among the Haida was twelve or thirteen years old, her aunt or grandmother took her to some quiet place along the seashore; there she pierced a little hole in the lower lip of the child, using a bit of sharp shell or stone. To keep the hole from closing when it healed, a bit of grass stalk was put into it. For a few days the place was sore, but it soon got well. The bit of stalk was then removed, and a little peg of wood put in. Later a larger peg or plug was inserted. When the girl had grown to be an old woman, she wore a large plug in her lower lip, which would hold it out flat almost like a shelf.

Many of the Northwest Coast tribes tattooed; generally the men were more marked with this than women. The patterns were usually animal figures, showing the man's family. The Haida were fond of having these queer pictures pricked into them. Upon their breasts they had the totem animal; on their arms other suitable patterns.

TATTOOING ON A HAIDA MAN.
(FROM MALLERY.)

The villages of these tribes are almost always on the seashore. The houses were generally in one long line, and all faced the sea. The houses of the different tribes differed somewhat. The house of the Haida was almost square, measuring perhaps forty or fifty feet on a side. In olden times they were sunk several feet into the ground.   On entering the house the visitor found himself upon a platform several feet wide running around the four sides; from it he stepped down upon a second platform, and from it upon a central square of dirt which contained the fireplace.   The eating place was around this hearth; the place for lounging, visiting, and sleeping was

GOLD CHIEF'S HOUSE, QUEEN CHARLOTTE'S ISLAND. (FROM PHOTOGRAPH.)

on the upper platform.   There each person of the household had his or her own place.   At its rear edge, near the wall, were boxes containing the person's treasures and the household's food.   There was but one doorway and no windows in a Haida house.   Outside the house, at the middle of the front, stood a curious, great, carved post of wood. These were covered with queer animal and bird

patterns, each with some meaning (see XXIX.).
In Haida houses the doorway was cut in the
lower part of this great post or pole.

The beach in front of the village used to be
covered with canoes dragged up on the sand.
These canoes were "dugouts" of single tree
trunks. The logs were cut in summer time, the
best wood being yellow cedar. The chief tool
used was the adze, made of stone or shell. Fire
was used to char the wood to be cut away. After
it had been partly cut out inside it was stretched
or shaped by steaming with water and hot stones,
and then putting in stretchers. Sometimes single-
log canoes were large enough to carry from thirty
to sixty people. They were often carved and
painted at the ends. The paddles used in driving these canoes were rather slender and long-
bladed, often painted with designs.

The present dress of these Indians is largely
the same as our own. In the days of the first
voyagers, they wore beautiful garments of native
manufacture. They had quantities of fine furs
of seals and sea-otters. These were worn as
blankets; when not in use they were carefully
folded and laid away in boxes. They wore close
and fine blankets of the wool of the mountain
sheep and the hair of the mountain goat. These
were closely woven and had a fine long fringe
along the lower border. They were covered with
patterns representing the totem animals. The
blanket itself was a dirty white in color, but

the designs were worked in black, yellow, or
brown. Further south, among the Tshimpshian
Indians of British Columbia, fine blankets were
woven of the soft and flexible inner bark of the
cedar; these were bordered with strips of fur.

These Indians still wear the ancient hat.
Among the southern tribes it is made of cedar

BLANKET: CHILCAT INDIANS, ALASKA. (FROM NIBLACK.)

bark, and is soft and flimsy. In the north it is
made of spruce or other roots, and is firm and
unyielding. The shape of the lower part of the
hat is a truncated cone. Among the Tlingit and
Haida this is surmounted by a curious, tall cylin-
der, which is divided into several joints, or seg-
ments, called *skil*. The number of these shows
the importance of the wearer.

The food of these tribes came largely from the sea. Fish were speared, trapped, and caught with hook and line. For halibut, queer, large, wooden hooks were used. When the fish had been drawn to the surface, they were killed with wooden spears. Both hooks and spears were curiously carved. Flesh of larger fishes, like halibut and salmon, was dried in the sun or over fire, and packed away. Clams were dried and strung on sticks. Seaweed was dried and pressed into great, square flat

HALIBUT HOOKS OF WOOD. (FROM ORIGINALS IN PEABODY MUSEUM.)

cakes; so were berries and scraped cedar bark. The people were fond of oil, and got it from many different fish. The most prized was that of the oolachen or candle-fish. This fish is so greasy that when put into a frying-pan, there is soon nothing left but some bones and scales floating about in the grease! To get this oil, the little fish were thrown into a canoe full of water. This was heated with stones made very hot in a fire, and then dropped into it. The heat drove out the oil, which floated on the top and was skimmed off

and put into natural bottles — tubes of hollow
seaweed stalk. At all meals a dish of oil stood
in the midst of the party, and bits of dried fish,
seaweed cake, or dried bark were dipped into it
before being eaten.

XXVIII.

SOME RAVEN STORIES.

ALL the Northwest Coast tribes had many
stories. Some of these stories had been borrowed
from tribe to tribe, and were told at many different
places. Usually, however, the single tribes had
stories that were favorites with them and really belonged to them. The favorite stories among the
Tlingit and Haida were about the raven, whom
they called *yetl*. There were many stories told of
him and his doings. It is difficult sometimes to
tell just what yetl was—whether bird or man. He
could take on many forms, and was usually the
friend of the Indians. In the olden time they
did not have fire, daylight, fresh water, or the
oolachen fish. It was yetl, the raven, called also
Nekilstlas, who got them these good things.

All of these precious things belonged to a
great chief who had a lovely daughter. The
raven made love to this maiden. Once when at
their house he pretended to be thirsty and begged
her for a drink of water. The girl brought it to

him in a bucket. He drank a little and laid the rest aside. By and by every one in the house was fast asleep except the raven; he was watching. He then got up quietly, put on his feather coat, took up the bucket in his bill and flew away with it. He was in such a hurry that he spilled the water here and there, and where it fell there have since been rivers and lakes. Never since that time have the Indians been without water.

But it was much harder to get the fire. Nekilstlas no longer dared to go to the chief's house or to make love to the maiden. He, however, changed himself into a spruce needle and floated on the water. He was thus got into the house without any one's knowing it, and there he changed into a little boy baby, whom the girl treated like her own son. He stayed there a long time, waiting his chance. At last, one day, he seized a burning brand from the fire and flew out of the smoke-hole in the roof with it. He was so careless that he set fire to many things. At the north end of Vancouver Island many of the trees are black, almost as if they were burned, and they say that was done by Nekilstlas when he flew away with the fire. However that may be, since then the Indians have had fire.

The old chief had the sun and the moon, but he kept them away from the people, and was very proud to think that he alone had light. Nekilstlas had to think a long time before he could make a plan to secure these for the Indians. At last he

made himself an imitation sun and put on it
something which made it shine. He then taunted
the chief by telling him that he too had a light.
For a time the chief did not believe him. At last
Nekilstlas drew back his feather coat and let a
piece of his bogus sun be seen. The chief believed it, and was so angry that he placed his real
sun and moon in the sky, where they have been
lights to the Indians ever since.

The last of the four possessions which the
raven wanted to get from the old chief for his
human friends was the oolachen fish, which yields
the oil of which the Indians are so fond. The
shag is a dirty seaside bird that has the unpleasant habit of vomiting up its food when it is
excited. He was, however, a special friend of the
chief, and one of the few whom he used to invite
to eat oolachen with him. One time the shag had
been eating pretty heartily at the chief's house,
and afterward the raven set him and the sea-gull
to fighting. In his excitement the shag threw
up the fish he had eaten. The raven took the
scales and smeared himself and his canoe all over
with them. Going then to the chief's house, he
asked if he might come in and rest, that he was
tired out from catching oolachen. The chief
thought at first that he was telling a lie, but when
he saw the scales, he thought there must be other
oolachen besides his, and in his rage he opened
the boxes in which he kept them and let them all
loose. Since then the Indians have had abun-

dance of the oolachen to give them the oil they need.

Besides these stories of the things the raven got for them, there are others. The raven is not always the friend of men, and sometimes he does them harm and not good. There is a story of the raven and the fisherman. This fisherman had much trouble from some one stealing the bait and fish from his fish-hook. The thief was no one else than the raven. The fisherman finally put a magic hook on his line and let it down. When the raven tried to steal from this he was caught. When he had been pulled up to the surface of the water, he struggled fearfully, by pressing against the canoe with his feet and his wings. The fisherman, however, was too strong for him. He pulled so hard that he tore the raven's beak off, and then, seizing him, dragged him in shore. When he pulled off the raven's beak, the bird turned into a man, but he kept his face so covered up with his feather garment that only his eyes could be seen. The fisherman could not make him uncover his face; but one young man who stood by picked up a handful of dirt and rubbed it into the raven's eyes. Smarting with pain and taken by surprise, the raven threw off his mantle, and the men saw who he was. The raven was so angry, that ever since then ravens and their friends, the crows, have constantly troubled fishermen.

The Tshimpshian, who live south of the Tlingit,

on the mainland, have a story of the raven. They
say that two boys lived in a village. One of them
was the son of a chief. One day the chief's son
said to the other, when they were playing, " Let
us take skins of birds and fly up to heaven."
They did so, and found things up there quite like
this world. They found a house there, near a
pond of water; and in this house lived a chief,
who was a sort of deity. The daughters of this
deity caught the two boys and were finally married
to them, although the deity did not like them, and
tried in every way to do them harm. They always
escaped, however. They lived together there for
a long time, and at last the wife of the chief's son
had a little boy baby. One day, when she was
playing with the baby, the little one slipped out
of her hands, and fell down, down, from the sky
into the sea. It happened that it was found and
saved by the chief, who was really the baby's
grandfather, though no one knew it at the time.
When the little one had been taken to the village,
it would not, for some time, eat anything. They
offered it salmon and berry cake and hemlock
bark, but he would not touch any of them. At
last his grandfather said, " Feed him some fish
stomachs." Then the little fellow began to eat
very greedily, and before he got through he had
eaten up all the food that the village had stored
away for use. Then he surprised every one by
saying, " Don't you know who I am? I am the
raven."

INDIAN CARRIER: ALASKA. (FROM KRAUSE.)

But the stories of the raven, if they were all written out, would make a large book. The naughty, greedy, dirty bird was the great hero of these peoples. They were anxious to explain everything, and most of their stories are to tell how things came to be.

Many persons have made collections of the stories of the Northwest Coast tribes. Boas, Chamberlain, Niblack, and Deans are among them.

XXIX.

TOTEM POSTS.

On approaching villages of many tribes on the Northwest Coast, the traveler sees great numbers of carved wooden posts. The largest, most striking, and most curious are no doubt those of the Tlingit of Alaska, and the Haida of Queen Charlotte Islands. Some of these posts stand in front of the houses, or very near them; others are set near the beach, beyond the village. When old they are weather-beaten and gray. They are sometimes compared to a forest of tree trunks left after a fire has swept through a wooded district.

There are three kinds of these carved posts, — totem posts, commemorative posts, and death posts. The death posts are the simplest of the three. Among the Tlingit and Haida the dead were usually burned. If the man had been important, a display was made of his body. He was dressed in his finest clothing, and all his treasures were placed around him. People came for some days to see his riches. At last the day for the burning of his body arrived. Many persons were present. The faces of the mourners were blackened, their hair cut short, and their heads were sprinkled with eagle-down. After the body had been burned, the ashes were gathered and

CHIEF'S HOUSE: QUEEN CHARLOTTE'S INLET. (FROM PHOTOGRAPH.)

put into a box, which was placed in a cavity hollowed out in the lower part of the death post. This was the old custom; nowadays the ashes may be put somewhere else. At the top of the death post was a cross-board on which was carved or painted the totem of the dead man.

The second kind of carved post is the commemorative post, put up to celebrate some important event. An old chief named Skowl once erected a great post near his house. He had erected it to commemorate the failure of the Russian missionaries to convert his village to Christianity. When the last missionary had gone, he put it up to recall their failure and to ridicule their religion. It was curiously carved. At the top was an eagle; below it a man with his right hand lifted, pointing to the sky; below it an angel; then a priest with his hands crossed upon his breast; then an eagle; lastly a trader.

The totem posts are, however, the most interesting. They are taller, more carefully made, and more elaborately carved than the others. They stand in front of the houses; among Tlingit at one side, among Haida at the very middle and close to the house. In fact, among the Haida the doorway of the house was a hole cut through the lower end of the totem post. The carvings on these posts refer to the people living in the house. Thus, in one Haida totem post there was a brown bear at the top — the totem of the man of the house; next came four *skil* or divisions of a hat; then came the great raven; then the bear and the hunter; then a bear — the last being the totem of the woman of the house.

Among the Tlingit and Haida every one bears the name of some animal or bird. Thus, among the Tlingit there are eighteen great families, with the name of wolf, bear, eagle, whale, shark, porpoise, puffin, orca, orca-bear; raven, frog, goose, beaver, owl, sea-lion, salmon, dogfish, crow. The first nine of these are considered related to one another; so are the last nine related. A man may not marry a woman of his own animal name or totem; nor can he marry one of the related families. Thus a wolf man could not marry a woman who was a wolf, or an eagle, or a shark, but he might marry a raven or a frog.

With us a child takes its father's name, but with these people it takes its mother's name. If a bear man married a raven woman, all the children would be ravens. The animal whose name a man bears is his *totem*. There is always some story told by people as to how they came to have their totem. Every one believes that the animal that is his totem can help him, and he pays much respect to it.

One story of how the bear became a totem is as follows: Long, long ago an Indian went into the mountains to hunt mountain goats. When far from home he met a black bear who took him home with him, and taught him to build boats and catch salmon. The man stayed two years

with the bear, and then went home to his village.
Every one feared him, for they thought him a
bear; he looked just like one. One man, however, caught him and took him home to his house.
He could not speak, and could not eat cooked
food. A great medicine man advised that he
should be rubbed with magic herbs. When this
was done, he became a man again. After that,
whenever he wanted anything, he went out into
the woods and found his bear friend, who always
helped him. What the bear taught him was of
great use to him, and he caught plenty of salmon
in the winter time when the river was covered
with ice. The man built a fine new house, and
painted the picture of a bear upon it. His sister
made him a new dancing blanket, and into it she
wove a picture of a bear. Ever since then the
descendants of that man's sister have the bear for
their totem.

Now you see something of the meaning of the
totem posts. Upon them are carved the totems
of the people living in the house. They are a
great doorplate, giving the names of the family.
This is important, because among Indians all the
persons who have the same totem must help one
another. If a man were in trouble, it was the
duty of his totem-fellows to aid him. If he were
a stranger, it was their duty to receive him. When
a Tlingit or Haida found himself in a strange
village, his first care would be to examine the
totem posts to find one that bore his own totem.

At the house marked by it he would surely be welcome.

But it was a rare thing for a totem post to have only the figures of the totems of the man and his wife. Other designs were carved in between these. These other designs might tell of the man's wealth or his importance, or they might represent some family story. The people of every

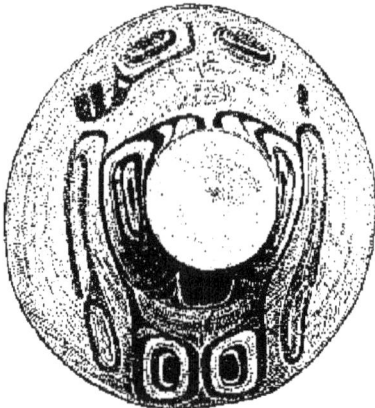

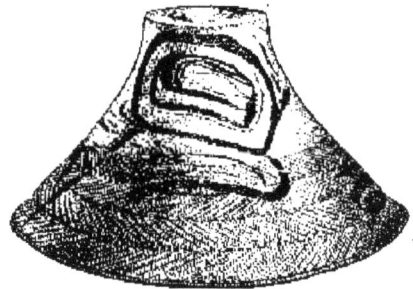

HAT OF NORTHWEST COAST, TOP VIEW.   HAT OF NORTHWEST COAST, SIDE VIEW.
(FROM ORIGINAL IN PEABODY MUSEUM.)   (FROM ORIGINAL IN PEABODY MUSEUM.)

totem had many stories which belonged only to them. In the totem post, already described, probably the great raven, and the bear, and the hunter, represented such stories. The four *skil* probably indicated that the man was important, for a man's importance is shown by the number of *skil* in his hat. The carving at the bottom, however, was most significant, for it gave the name of the woman and all her children.

ALBERT P. NIBLACK, of the United States navy, has written *The Coast Indians of Southern Alaska and Northern British Columbia.*

XXX.

INDIANS OF CALIFORNIA.

NOWHERE among American Indians are more languages found in a smaller space than in California. Those spoken near the Coast, within the area of the Missions, appear to belong to at least nine language families or stocks. In Powell's map the state looks like a piece of patchwork, so many are the bits of color, which represent different languages. These Coast Indians of California were ugly to see. They were of medium stature, awkwardly shaped, with scrawny limbs; they had dull faces, with fat and round noses, and looked much like negroes, only their hair was straight. In disposition they were said to be sluggish, indolent, cowardly, and unenterprising. Some tribes in the interior were better, but none of the California Indians seem to have presented a high physical type or much comfort in life.

We shall say little about the life and customs of the California Indians, and what we do say will be chiefly about the Coahuilla tribe. These Indians live in the beautiful high Coahuilla Valley in Southern California. Formerly at least part of the tribe were " Mission Indians." Some of them were connected with the San Gabriel Mission near the present city of Los Angeles. They appear to present a better type than many of the Mission Indians, being larger, better built, and stronger. Ramona, who was the heroine of Helen Hunt Jackson's story, is a Coahuilla Indian, still living. If she ever was beautiful, it

GRANARY AT COAHUILLA. (FROM PHOTOGRAPH.)

must have been long ago, although she is not an old woman. These Indians live in little houses, largely built of brush, scattered over the valley. They have some ponies and cattle, and cultivate some ground. Near every house, perched upon big boulders, are quaint little structures made of woven willows and like big beehives in form; they are granaries for stowing away acorns or grain.

Acorns are much used by California Indi
They are bitter and need to be sweete
They are first pounded to a meal or flour.
wide basket is filled with sand, which is c
fully scooped away so as to leave a basin-sha
surface; the acorn meal is spread upon
and water is poured upon it. The bitternes
soaked out, and the meal left sweet and goo

COILED BASKETS: CALIFORNIA. (FROM PHOTOGRAPH.)

A fine art among most Californian tribes is
making of baskets. Those made at Coah
are mostly what is known as "coiled wc
A bunch of fine, slender grass is taken
treated as if it were a rope. It is coiled aro
and around in a close coil. Long strips of
grass are then taken and wrapped like a th
around the coiled rope, sewing the coil at e

wrapping to the next coil. In this way the foundation coiled rope of grass is entirely covered and concealed by the wrapping of reed grass, and at the same time firmly united. By using differently colored strips of the reed grass, patterns are worked in. Horses, men, geometrical patterns, and letters are common. Among some Californian tribes such baskets were covered with brilliant feathers, which were woven in during the making.

Among the delicacies of some south Californian tribes was roasted mescal. Mescal is a plant of the desert, with great, pointed, fleshy leaves. At the proper time it throws up a huge flower-stalk, which bears great numbers of flowers. Mr. Lummis describes the roasting of its leaves and stalks: "A pit was dug, and a fire of the greasewood's crackling roots kept up therein until the surroundings were well heated. Upon the hot stones of the pit was laid a layer of the pulpiest sections of the mescal; upon this a layer of wet grass; then another layer of mescal, and another of grass, and so on. Finally the whole pile was banked over with earth. The roasting — or, rather, steaming — takes from two to four days. . . . When he banks the pile with earth, he arranges a few long bayonets of the mescal so that their tips shall project. When it seems to him that the roast should be done, he withdraws one of these plugs. If the lower end is well done, he uncovers the heap and proceeds to feast; if still too rare, he possesses his soul in patience until a later experiment proves the baking." This method of roasting mescal is about the same pursued farther north with camas root.

A gambling game common among Californian tribes is called by the Spanish name *peon*. It is very similar to a game played in many other parts of the United States by many Indian tribes. It consists simply of guessing in which of two hands the marked one of two sticks or objects is held. The game is played by two parties, one of which has the sticks, while the other guesses. Each success is marked by a stick or counter for the winner, and ten counts make a game. Among the Coahuillas there are four persons on a side. Songs are sung, which become loud and wild; at times the players break into fierce barking. Then the guess is made. Great excitement arises, which grows wilder and wilder toward the end of a close game. Violent movements and gestures are made to deceive the carefully watching guessers. Sometimes men will bet on this game the last things they own, even down to the clothes they wear.

Mr. Barrows, who has described the game of *peon* tells of the bird dances of the Coahuillas. These Indians highly regard certain birds. Of all, the eagle is chief. In the eagle dance the dancer wears a breech-clout; his face, body, and limbs are painted in red, black, and white; his dance skirt and dance bonnet are made of eagle feathers. In his dancing and whirling he imitates the circling and movements of the eagle. At times he whirls about the great circle of spectators so rapidly that his feather skirt stands up straight below his arms. The music of this dance is so old that the words are not understood even by the singers.

The story of the Missions in California is a most

MISSION OF SANTA BARBARA, CALIFORNIA. (FROM PHOTOGRAPH.)

interesting one. You remember that California was a part of New Spain; when Mexico rebelled against Spain and gained her independence, California was a part of the new republic. The Spanish government gave California over to the Jesuits to develope. They took possession in 1697 and built a Mission at San Dionisio, in Lower California. By 1745, they had fourteen Missions established, all in what is now Lower California. The Jesuits gave way to the Fran-

ciscan monks, and these began in 1769 their first
Mission in California proper, at San Diego.   One
after another was added, until, in 1823, there were
twenty-one Franciscan Missions, stretching from
San Diego to San Francisco.   Each mission had
a piece of ground fifteen miles square.   The
center of the Mission was the church, with clois-
ters where the monks lived.   The houses of the
Indian converts — which were little huts — were
grouped together about the church, arranged in
rows.   Unmarried men were housed in a separate
building or buildings, as were young women
also.   During the sixty-five years of these Missions about seventy-nine thousand converts were
made.   Every one at these Missions was busy.
The men kept the flocks and herds, sheared the
sheep, and cared for the fields and vines.   Women
cared for the houses and the church.   There was
spinning, weaving, leather work, and plenty else
to be done.   Still the Indians were not hard
worked, and they ought to have been happy.
Their time was regularly planned out for them.
At sunrise all rose and went to mass; soon after
mass breakfast was ready and sent to the houses
in baskets; then every one worked.   At noon
dinner was sent around again from house to
house; then came the afternoon work.   After
evening mass, there was a supper of sweet gruel.
There was a good deal of time left after the
services and work were through.   The monks
allowed the Indians to keep up their native dances

and amusements so far as they believed them harmless.

Some persons seem to think that the monks made slaves of the Indians. Rather they considered them children, who needed oversight, direction, and sometimes punishment. However, the Indians were probably better dressed and housed and fed than ever before, and, perhaps, happier. But the Missions are now past. Their twenty-one old churches still stand, — our most interesting historical relics, — but the Indian converts have scattered, and in time they will forget, if they have not already forgotten, that they or their people were ever Mission Indians.

XXXI.

THE AZTECS.

WHEN the Spaniards reached Mexico, that country was filled with Indians belonging to many different tribes. These differed in language and in customs. Perhaps the most powerful and warlike tribe was that of the Aztecs, who lived in the central high table-land, with a chief city named Tenochtitlan. This city, occupying the same site as the present city of Mexico, was situated upon the shores of, and partly within, the lake of Texcoco. The lake lay in a beautiful valley which was occupied not only by the Aztecs, but also by a number of other tribes related to them in speech. Among these tribes were the Acolhuas, with their chief city of Texcoco, and the Tecpanecans, whose chief city was Tlacopan.

These three tribes spoke about the same language, and, after a great deal of quarreling among themselves, they united in a league or confederacy something like that of the Iroquois. Together, they were so strong that they carried on successful war against their neighbors. When they conquered a tribe, they did not take its land away nor interfere with its government, but compelled the people to pay an annual tribute to the confederacy. At the head of the confederacy was a great war-chief, who was called by the title of the Chief of Men. When Cortez conquered Mexico, the name of this "Chief of Men" was Montezuma.

The Aztecs raised crops of corn, beans, squashes, and chili peppers. Still they got a considerable amount of food from hunting, and they knew how to make snares and traps for capturing animals. Their lake used to be covered with ducks, and to capture these they employed a clever trick. Calabashes are large gourds. The Aztec hunters left calabashes floating at places where ducks were plenty so that the birds should be used to seeing them, and pay no attention to them. When a man wished to catch ducks, he placed a big calabash over his head, and waded cautiously out into the water until it was just deep enough for it to look as if his calabash were floating. Little by little, he moved over toward the swimming

ducks, and, when among them, he seized one by
the legs and dragged it under water; then another,
and another, and so on.   Ducks were not the only
food taken from the lake.   The scum or dirt floating on the water was skimmed off, and pressed
into cakes; the eggs of a fly, which were laid in
bunches on the rushes, near, or in the water, were
gathered and eaten.   These eggs are still a favorite food with modern Mexicans.

The Aztecs knew how to spin and weave.
They had cotton, and they also had a fine, stout
fiber from the maguey plant.   From these they
made good cloths which they sometimes dyed in
bright colors.   The dress of the men consisted of
a sort of blanket or cloak — worn knotted over
one shoulder — and the breech-clout.   The women
wore a skirt, which was only a long strip of cloth
wrapped around the body, and held firmly in place
by a belt; they also wore a pretty sleeveless waist.
Men wore sandals on the feet, but usually went
bareheaded.   Great officials, however, were finely
dressed, and one might tell from the clothing
what official he met.   Men often wore lip-stones.
These were in idea like the lip-plugs of the Haida
women, but were different in shape and material.
Most of them were made of obsidian, — a fine-
grained, glassy, black mineral.   Their shape was
that of a little stovepipe hat.   The brim was
inside the lip and prevented the stone from slip-
ping out; the crown projected from the hole in
the lower lip.

The common people lived in huts made of mud or other destructible material; but the buildings intended for the government and for religion were sometimes grand affairs, built of stone and covered with plaster. This plastering was sometimes white, sometimes red, and upon it were at times pictures painted in brilliant colors. These pictures generally represented warriors ready for battle, or priests before the altar. Temples were usually built upon flat-topped pyramids. These were often large, and were terraced on one or more sides. Sometimes they were coated with plaster. Flights of steps, or sloping paths, led to the summit. There would be found the temple and the gods. The gods of the Aztecs were like the Aztecs themselves, bloodthirsty and cruel.

In war the Aztecs used clubs, wooden swords, bows and arrows, spears or darts, slings and stones. They had wooden swords with broad, flat blades, grooved along the sides; into these grooves were cemented sharp pieces of obsidian. These were fearful weapons until dulled or broken by use. Spears and darts were often thrown with a wooden stick or hurler called an *atlatl*. Important warriors carried round or rectangular shields upon their left arms to ward off attack. These shields often bore patterns worked in bright feathers. Sometimes the whole dress of warriors was covered with feathers, and famous braves wore helmets of wood on their heads, from which rose great masses of fine feathers. Often warriors wore a sort of jacket covering the upper part of the body and reaching the knees. This was padded thickly with cotton, and arrows shot with great force could hardly penetrate it.

CALENDAR STONE. (FROM PHOTOGRAPH.)

In battle the Aztecs did not desire to kill the enemy, but preferred to capture prisoners to sac-. rifice to the gods. When a man was captured he was very well treated until the day for his sacrifice came. He was taken up to the temple on the pyramid and thrown on his back upon a sacrificial stone. He was held by several priests, while the high priest, with a knife of stone, cut open his breast. The heart was torn out, and offered to the gods; some other parts were cut off for them or for the priests. The rest of the body was then thrown down to the soldier who had captured the victim, and who waited below. He and his friends bore it away and ate it, or parts of it, as a religious duty. All the time the sacrifices were being made, the great drum was beaten. It made a mournful noise that could be heard to a great distance. In the National Museum in the city of Mexico is a great carved stone which is believed by many persons to be one of these old sacrificial stones upon which victims were sacrificed.

STONE IDOL: MEXICO. (FROM PHOTOGRAPH.)

In the same museum is a great stone idol. It was dug up about a hundred years ago in the central square of the city of Mexico. It probably stood in the great temple of the old Aztecs, which was totally destroyed by Cortez and his soldiers when they finally captured the city of Tenochtitlan. What an ugly thing it is! It is more than eight feet high and more than five feet across, but is cut from a single block of stone. It has a head in front, and another one behind; they look something like serpent heads. While the general form of this great idol is human, it has neither the feet nor hands of a man. The skirt it wears is made of an intertwined mass of rattle-snakes. A human skull is at the front of the belt. Four human hands apparently severed from their bodies are displayed upon the chest. This is only one of many curious and dreadful Aztec gods.

It would take a book larger than this to describe the Aztecs properly. It would take another to describe the conquest of Mexico by the Spaniards. Cortez had only a handful of men to fight against many thousands. But he had guns, powder, and horses, all of which were unknown before to the Aztecs and which they greatly feared. Sometime you must read Bernal Diaz del Castillo's story of the Conquest. He was one of Cortez's soldiers. He tells us that he was present in one hundred and nineteen battles and engagements. He also says: " Of the five hundred and fifty soldiers, who left the island of Cuba with Cortez, at the moment I am writing this history in the year one thousand five hundred and sixty-eight, no more than five are living, the rest having been killed in the wars, sacrificed to idols, or died naturally."

XXXII.

THE MAYAS AND THE RUINED CITIES OF YUCATAN AND CENTRAL AMERICA.

OF all North American tribes the Mayas were perhaps the most advanced in culture, the nearest to civilization. They lived in the peninsula of Yucatan and in the adjacent states of Tabasco and Chiapas in Mexico, and in Honduras and Guatemala in Central America. While true Mayas did *not* occupy the whole of this district, it was practically occupied by them and peoples speaking languages closely related to theirs.

There are many Mayas now alive. It is a common but serious mistake to imagine that Aztecs, Mayas, and other tribes of Mexico and Central America at the time of the Conquest are extinct. Many tribes have died out; but the famous Aztecs and Mayas are still numerous. The Mayas to-day are short, well-built, broad-shouldered peoples with unusually dark skin. They have much energy and are notable for their independent spirit. Within the last few years they have given the Mexican government much trouble. They have not given up their own language, but have learned to write it, and a considerable number of books and papers have been printed in it. They retain their ancient dress to some degree. Almost every one who sees the modern Mayas speaks well of them, — as clean, neat, straightforward, and reliable.

It is not the Mayan peoples of to-day, but those of the past, of whom we desire to speak. They were the best builders in North America, and the ruins of their cities testify to their skill. More than fifty years ago, John L. Stephens, with an artist named Catherwood, traveled in Honduras, Guatamala, Chiapas, and Yucatan. Mr. Stephens described their travels and the ruins they explored, and Mr. Catherwood drew pictures of them. Americans were astonished at these researches. These travelers visited forty ruins of ancient cities in Yucatan alone. Since that time many other travelers have been there, and much is known of Mayan architecture.

Most of the ruins appear to be those of buildings intended for governmental or religious purposes. Few, if any, were houses for individuals. Probably these fine, large buildings were at the center of towns, the dwelling houses of which were frail huts of poles, branches, canes, etc. These have disappeared, leaving no sign of their former existence. All through Mexico, to-day, in Indian towns, the only permanent constructions which would leave ruins are the church and the town house. Everything else is frail hut.

Nearly every one of these old towns presents some peculiarity of interest. We can, however, only briefly describe three. *Palenque* appears to be one of the oldest. It is in the most southern state of Mexico, Chiapas. The more important ruins are those of the " palace " and five temples near it. The buildings were all raised upon terrace platforms; they were long and narrow; the walls were thick, and built of stones and mud, with cement. The walls were faced with slabs of stone, often carved with figures of gods, hieroglyphic characters, etc. Usually two long corridors ran lengthwise, side by side, through the building. These open upon the supporting platform by a line of rectangular doorways of uniform size. There were no true arches, but the corridors had pyramidal arched vaultings. The roof went up from all four sides, at a low and then at a sharper angle. A curious crest or roof-comb surmounted the roof. Much plastering was used in these buildings; the walls were sometimes thickly and smoothly covered. Stucco figures were worked upon some of the walls. One temple, called the " Temple of the Beau Relief," had a great tablet of stucco work, with the figure of a man seated upon a sort of rounded stone seat; he wore a coiled cap, with great waving plumes. His hands were making some sort of signs; he wore a necklace of beads, with a pendant carved with a human face. The stone upon which he sits is supported on a bench, the arms at the ends of which are lion heads, and the supports of which are four heavily carved, but well-made, lion feet. In other temples there were tablets of carved stone. Two of these are famous. One represents the sun, as

a human face, placed upon two crossed shafts;
on either side of this central object stands a profile figure, one of which appears to represent a
priest, the other a worshiper. Both stand on
curiously bent human figures. In the second
tablet, two similar figures are shown, but they
stand at the two sides of a cross, upon which
perches a bird. On these tablets of the sun and
cross are many curious hieroglyphs forming an
inscription.

Copan in Honduras is another famous location
of ruins left by some Mayan people. The most
interesting objects there are great stone statues
or figures with stone altars before them. These
statues are taller than a man and are cut from
single blocks of stone. They differ so much in
face and dress that they have been believed by
some writers to be portraits. The persons are
usually beautifully dressed and ornamented. They
wear beads, pendants, tassels, belts, ear ornaments, and headdresses. The headdresses are
usually composed of great feathers. The sides
and sometimes the back of these figures are covered with hieroglyphics of the same kind as those
at Palenque. The "altars" in front of these
stone figures, differ in form and size, but are cut
from single blocks of stone. One which is
nearly square has at the sides a series of figures
of human beings sitting cross-legged; there are
four of these on each side, or sixteen in all.

At *Chichen Itza*, the buildings are remark-

le for the mass of carved stone work
nich they are decorated, outside and in
reat horrid masks, geometrical patterns, i
'ined snakes, occur. At some corners of b
gs are curious hook-like projections, w
me persons have thought were meant to r

RUINED BUILDING AT CHICHEN ITZA. (AFTER STEPHENS.)

nt elephant trunks. Mr. Holmes desc
refully carved pillars resting upon gig
ake-head carvings. One room in the " Te
the Tigers " has the inside wall compose
ocks of stone, each of which is sculptured.
rvings represent persons richly dressed. V

the building was first made, these figures were
brightly painted and traces of the colors still
remain.

We can tell a good deal about the lives of the
builders of these old buildings from a study of the
figures and carvings. These show their dress and
modes of worship. The ruins themselves show
how they built. Figures on tablets at Palenque
show that they changed their head forms by ban‑
daging like some tribes of whom we know.

At Lorillard City, ruins explored by Mr. Char‑
nay, are some curious figures. Among them one
represents a person kneeling, with his tongue out,
and a cord passed through a hole in it. The old
Mayas really used to torture themselves this way
to please their gods. They pierced their tongues
and passed a rough cord through the hole, and
drew it back and forward.

No one can read the characters on the tablets
of Palenque and the stone figures at Copan. Sim‑
ilar characters occur at other ruins. At Tikal
some were cut upon beautiful wooden panels.
They were carved on greenstone ornaments,
scratched upon shells, and painted upon pottery.
There were plenty of books among the Mayas.
Some of these still exist, and four have been quite
carefully studied. They contain many quaint pic‑
tures of priests, gods, worshipers, etc. They also
contain many numbers and day names. There
are also in them many of the same strange hiero‑
glyphs, already mentioned. These are called

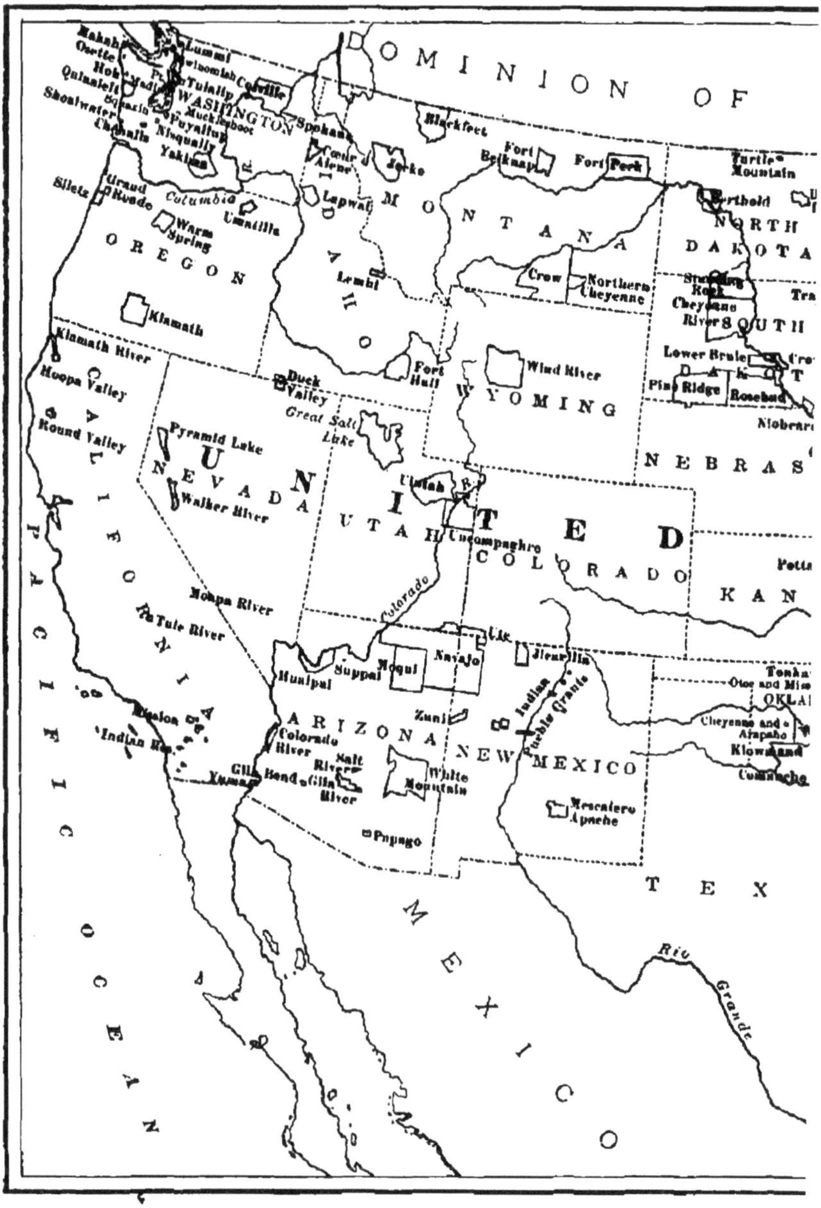
DOMINION OF
WASHINGTON
Makah
Ozette
Hoh
Quinaielt
Shoalwater
Chehalis
Lummi
Tulalip
Squaxin
Muckleshoot
Puyallup
Nisqually
Yakima
Colville
Spokane
Blackfeet
Fort Belknap
Fort Peck
Turtle Mountain
Jocko
MONTANA
Lapwai
IDAHO
Lemhi
Siletz
Grand Ronde
Columbia
Umatilla
Warm Spring
OREGON
Klamath
Berthold
NORTH DAKOTA
Standing Rock
Cheyenne River
SOUTH DAKOTA
Lower Brule
Pine Ridge
Rosebud
Niobrara
Crow
Northern Cheyenne
Wind River
WYOMING
Fort Hall
Duck Valley
Great Salt Lake
Klamath River
Hoopa Valley
Round Valley
CALIFORNIA
Pyramid Lake
NEVADA
Walker River
UNITED
UTAH
Uintah
Uncompahgre
COLORADO
Colorado
NEBRAS
KAN
Moapa River
Tule River
Mission
Indian Res.
Ute
Jicarilla
Navajo
Moqui
Suppai
Hualpai
ARIZONA
Zuni
Colorado River
Salt River
Gila River
Gila Bend
Yuma
White Mountain
Papago
NEW MEXICO
Pueblo Grande
Mescalero Apache
Otoe and Miss
OKLA
Cheyenne and Arapaho
Kiowa and
Comanche
TEX
Rio Grande
MEXICO
PACIFIC OCEAN

Map Showing
INDIAN RESERVATIONS
of the
UNITED STATES,
in 1897.

C A N A D A

MINNESOTA

Red Lake
Bois Forte
Vermilion L.
Deer Creek
Winnibigoshish
Leech Lake
Fond du Lac
Mille Lac
La Pointe
Lac Court Oreille
Lac du Flambeau
Menomonee
Stockbridge
WISCONSIN
Oneida

Grand Portage
Lake Superior
Red Cliff
L'Anse
Ontonagon

L. Michigan

OHIO

Isabella

Huron

Pottawatomie
of Huron

St. Lawrence R.
MAINE
VERMONT
N. HAMP.
MASS.
CONN.

Lake Ontario
Tuscarora
Tonawanda
Onondaga
Oneida
Cattaraugus
NEW YORK
Oil Spring
Allegany
Lake Erie

PENNSYLVANIA
N. J.
M.
D.
DEL.

WINNEBAGO
IOWA
Sac & Fox

ILLINOIS

INDIANA

OHIO

WEST VIRGINIA

VIRGINIA

UNITED STATES

Sac & Fox
Iowa

MISSOURI
Osage
Kaw
Kickapoo
Peoria
Ottawa
Miami
Shawnee
Wyandotte
Cherokee

KENTUCKY

TENNESSEE

NORTH CAROLINA
Qualla

ATLANTIC OCEAN

INDIAN TERRITORY
Choctaw
Red R.
Arkansas

ARKANSAS

MISSISSIPPI

ALABAMA

GEORGIA

SOUTH CAROLINA

LOUISIANA

FLORIDA

BAHAMA ISLANDS

G U L F   O F   M E X I C O

THE M.-N.CO., BUFFALO, N.Y.

"calculiform" or "pebble-shaped" characters, because they present a generally roundish outline,
as of a pebble cut through. It is plain that they
were at first simply pictures. Some of them, no
doubt, are still simple pictures of ideas; others
convey ideas different from those at first pictured;
many can no longer be seen to be pictures at all;
some, perhaps, represent sounds, and are not now
pictures for ideas. It is possible, in a general
way, to make out something of the sense of parts
of Mayan books and inscriptions, but it is quite
likely that they will never be exactly read as we
read our own written books.

XXXIII.

CONCLUSION.

An old Pani, in speaking of what was perhaps
the first official visit by whites to his tribe, said:
"I heard that long ago there was a time when
there were no people in this country except
Indians. After that the people began to hear of
men with white skins; they had been seen far to
the east. Before I was born they came to our
country and visited us. The man who came was
from the Government. He wanted to make a
treaty with us, and to give us presents—blankets
and guns and flint and steel and knives.
"The head chief told him that we needed none

of those things.   He said, ' We have our buffalo
and our corn.   These things the Ruler gave us,
and they are all that we need.   See this robe.
This keeps me warm in winter. I need no blanket.'

" The white men had with them some cattle,
and the chief said, ' Lead out a heifer here on
the prairie.'   They led her out, and the chief,
stepping up to her, shot her through behind the
shoulder with his arrow, and she fell down and
died.   Then the chief said, ' Will not my arrow
kill?   I do not need your guns.'   Then he took
his stone knife and skinned the heifer, and cut off
a piece of fat meat.   When he had done this, he
said, ' Why should I take your knives?   The
Ruler has given me something to cut with.'

" Then, taking the firesticks, he kindled a fire
to roast the meat; and while it was cooking, he
spoke and said, ' You see, my brother, that the
Ruler has given us all that we need: the buffalo
for food and clothing; the corn to eat with our
dried meat; bows, arrows, knives, and hoes — all
the implements that we need for killing meat or
for cultivating the ground.   Now go back to the
country from whence you came.   We do not want
your presents, and we do not want you to come
into our country.' "

And the old chief was right.   The Indians
were supplied with all they needed; what the
white man offered them was unnecessary, often it
was harmful.   They were happy and contented.
They were doing very well in their own way.

But the old times are gone. To-day the Indians
are few in number, and they are growing fewer.
There are many ingenious arguments to prove
the contrary. Three facts, however, are perfectly
plain. First, there were whole tribes that have
disappeared. The Beothuks and the Natchez
are but two tribes which are gone; such tribes
may be numbered by scores. Their names are
on record; their old locations are known; sometimes we have some knowledge of their customs
and ways, but *they* are dead. Secondly, many
tribes are rapidly dwindling. The Pani, between
1885 and 1889, a period of five years, fell from
one thousand and forty-five to eight hundred and
sixty-nine. When I knew the Tonkaways in the
Indian Territory, they numbered but thirty-five
persons, and had been disappearing at the rate of
one-third of the population in eight years. The
Haidas of Queen Charlotte Islands are becoming fewer. Dawson says: "One intelligent man
told me that he could remember the time —
which by his age could not have been more than
thirty years ago — when there was not room to
launch all the canoes of the village in a single
row, the whole length of the beach, when the
people set out on one of their periodical trading
expeditions to Port Simpson. The beach is about
half a mile long, and there must have been from
five to eight persons in each canoe." There are
to-day less than five hundred people in that village,
Skidgate. Thirdly, there are some tribes, like

the Cherokees and Sioux, which are large, prosperous, and wealthy. It is a money advantage to
belong to such tribes, and a great many men who
should be considered white men are counted with
such tribes and help to make them look as if they
were not dwindling. It is quite certain that true
Indians of pure blood are rapidly diminishing.

The whites have brought them whisky, which
has killed thousands. They have brought vices
and diseases which have swept off thousands
more. They have put an end to the old free,
open-air life. They have taught them unwhole-
some means of cookery that cause scrofula and
other diseases. They have taught them to build
close, stuffy houses, which cause consumption
which is fearfully destructive to the Indians. It
seems to make little difference whether it is an
open foe with the whisky bottle, or an apparent
friend with money for a "civilized home" ("a nice,
comfortable, little house") who comes; the white
man's touch destroys the Indians.

Whether the Indians really die out or not, their
old life will surely disappear. One after another
many of the things we have here read of together
have disappeared. Others will soon die out. The
houses, dress, weapons, games, dances, ceremonials, will go. It is only a matter of time. But
they ought always to be interesting to us as
Americans.

The condition of the Indians to-day is a sad
and pathetic one. They may all echo the words

of Red Jacket. They have been crowded upon by the white man's hunger for land until now they have little left. Not long ago they held the continent; to-day they are almost prisoners upon a few patches of land called reservations. They are secure of these only until the white man wants them. Time after time Indians have given up their lands and removed to distant places because their old homes were wanted by white men. Every time they have been promised that in their new homes they should be undisturbed. Yet whenever, in their onward march, white men came to be neighbors, the old troubles came again. Encroachment, aggression, then perhaps open warfare, and then, another removal. Helen Hunt Jackson's *Century of Dishonor* tells only a part of the story. Every boy and girl in the United States should read it.

Here on a map you see the present location of most of the Indians. The reservations vary in size and in quality. Some of them have little that can attract the whites. In these the Indians may be left in peace. The present idea of what to do with the Indians is shown by the Dawes Bill. This is apparently a benevolent scheme for happily settling the Indians on individual farms. Imagine a reservation belonging to some tribe. A part of the reservation is cultivated by the more progressive Indians. The rest is not used except perhaps for hunting or fishing, or wandering over. The whole belongs to the tribe absolutely, and we have promised that it shall never be taken away from them. But now the Dawes Bill is passed. It is said, a little farm apiece is all that is necessary for these Indians. It would be much better to give each of them just what he needs and then to buy the balance of the land (cheap of course), and give it to white people. Whenever the Indians agree to it, we will divide up the land, allot each his land in severalty, and the Indian problem is solved. All this sounds very well, but it is enough to make one's heart bleed to see the way in which it is carried out. Many times the Indians do not wish to take their land in severalty. Certainly they ought not to be forced to do so against their will. Yet commission after commission, special agent after special agent, is sent to tribes to persuade, beg, and harass them into accepting allotment. Many times half threats are made; hints are vaguely thrown out as to what may happen if they don't take their little farms and sell the balance of their reservation. Surveyors are hired to go and survey within the reservation so as to make the Indians think their land will be taken away anyway. At last the poor harassed tribe yields. The men take their farms; they give up the balance of their land for a small price. Those who were industrious before take care of their land as they did before, no better, no worse. But the unprogressive Indian is not made industrious. He rents his land to some white man and spends his money in strong drink. As long as they were on the reservation there were laws to protect them from bad neighbors and whisky. But on his little farm the Indian may be next door to bad white men who sell him liquor whenever it is to their advantage.

There are many persons who think that missions and schools will make the Indians good and happy. So far as schools are concerned there are many. Some of them are simple day schools at the agency. Others are boarding schools still at the agency. Still others are great industrial schools at a town more or less distant. Of all these schools we think that those at the agency are the best kind. Such schools, well managed by thoroughly good teachers, ought to do the most good. They ought not to try to teach high branches, but to speak, read, and write English, a little arithmetic and a little knowledge of the great world. They ought to be industrial schools to the extent of teaching handiness in all the little things that need to be done about the house or the farm. They ought to aim to reach the parents and to interest them in their work. Progress in such schools is slow, but it is better for all to make a little progress, than for a few to get a great mass of information that they cannot use.

GLOSSARY.

OF INDIAN AND OTHER FOREIGN WORDS WHICH MAY NOT
READILY BE FOUND IN THE ENGLISH DICTIONARY.

The spellings of Indian words vary much with different authors:
in the following list the word as spelled in this book is first given,
then the pronunciation, then the number of a page on which the
meaning of the word will be found.

Single and combined consonants have their usual English
sounds except *c*, which is equal to *sh*; *s* is always as in *so*; final
s as in *gems* is represented by *z*; soft *g* is represented by *j*.

Vowels are as follows: —

a as in fat		ē as in meat		ō as in note	
ā " mane		i " pin		u " tub	
ä " father		ī " pine		ū " oo in spoon	
â " talk		o " not		oi " boil	
e " met					

Abalone [á-ba-lōn], 77.

Acolhua [ā-kōl'-wā], 209.

Adobé [a-dō'-bā], 163.

Algonkin [al-gón-kin], 108.

Alibamu [ál-i-ba-mū], 128.

Apache [a-pá-chā], 39.

Apalache [a-pā-lá-chā], 128.

Arapaho [ä-rá-pä-ho], 60.

Arickara [a-rí-kä-rä], 64.

Assinaboin, [a-sí-nä-boin], 57.

Athapaskan [äth'-ä-pás-kan], 3.

Atlatl [át-la-tl], 211.

Atotarho [át-ō-tä'r-hō], 116.

Aztec [az-tek], 208.

Beothuk [bē-ō'-thuk], 223.

Burro [bū'r-o], 91.

Busk [busk], 133.

Caddo [ká-dō], 134.

Cañon [kán-yun], 176.

Cassine [kás-sēn], 133.

Catolsta [ka-tō'l-stä], 144.

Cayuga [kā-yū-gä], 116.

Chelley [cā], 176.

Cherokee [che-rō-kē], 140.

Cheyenne [cī'-en], 60.

Chiapas [chē-á-pas], 215.

229

Chicasaw [chi-kä-så], 128.
Chichen Itza [chē'-chen ē'-tsu], 218.
Chilkat [chĬl-kat], 21.
Chinook [chi-nū'k], 182.
Choctaw [chók-tâ], 128.
Chunkey [chún-kā], 132.
Coahuilla [kō-wē'-yä], 201.
Cochiti [kō'-chē-tē'], 178.
Comanche [kō-mán-chē], 94.
Copan [kō-pan'], 218.
Corral [kō-rál], 165.
Coup [kū], 42.
Cree [krē], 108.
Creek [krēk], 128.
Estufa [es-tū-fä], 165.
Frijoles [frē-hō-lāz], 178 (means beans).
Glooskap [glōs-kap], 32.
Haida [hī-dä], 182.
Haliotis [ha-lē-ō-tis], 77.
Hano [hä-nō], 169.
Hayenwatha [hī-en-wä-thä], 116.
Hayoneta [hoi-ä-nā-tä], 145.
Hupa [hū'-pä], 76.
Itztapalapa [ēt's-tä-pä-lä'-pä], 55.
Kiowa [kī'-ō-wä], 60.
Kisi [kē'-sē], 170.
Kwakiutl [kwä'-kē-ū'tl], 182.
Lenape [le-nä'-pä], 109.
Lipan [lē-pan'], 56.
Maguey [ma-gä'], 71.
Mandan [man'-dan], 159.
Maya [mĭ'-yä], 215.
Mendoza [men-dō'-zä], 73.
Mesa [mā'-sä], 161.
Mescal [mes-cal'], 204.
Metate [mā-tä'-tä], 180.

Micam [mē'-câm], 66.
Miko [mē'-kō], 131.
Moki [mō'-kē], 168.
M'teoulin [m'tä-ū'-lin], 84.
Muskoki [mus-kō'-kē], 128.
Nanabush [na'-nä-būc], 112.
Navajo [na'vä-hō], 21.
Neeskotting [nē'-sko-ting], 51.
Nekilstlas [ne-kils'-tläs], 189.
Ojibwa [ō-jib'-wä], 108.
Oneida [ō-nī'-dä], 116.
Onondaga [on'-on-dä'-gä], 116.
Oolachen [ū'-la-chen], 191.
Oraibe [ō-rai'-bä], 169.
Otoe [ō'-tō], 92.
Pani [pâ-nē'], 60.
Pemmican [pĕ'-mi-kan], 57.
Pima [pē'-mä], 59.
Plaza [pla'-zä], 171.
Ponka [pon'-kä], 96.
Pueblo [pweb'-lō], 161.
Puskita [pus'-kē-tä], 133.
Rito [rē'-tō], 178 (means brook).
Sac [säc], 54.
Santee [San-tē'], 155.
Saponie [sa'-pō-nä], 119.
Seneca [se'-ne-kä], 116.
Senel [sä'-nel], 95.
Sequoyah [se-kwoi'-yä], 146.
Shawnee [câ-nē'], 107.
Shenanjie [ce-nan'-jä], 126.
Shonko [con'-kō], 151.
Shoshoné [co'-cō-nä'], 169.
Sioux [sū], 155.
Sipapu [sē-pä'-pū], 171.
Sisseton [si'-se-ton], 155.
Skil [skēl], 187.
Skowl [skōl], 197.

Succotash [su'-kō-tac], 56.
Tabasco [ta-bas'-kō], 215.
Taos [tows], 162.
Tecpanecan [tek'-pan-ē'-kan], 209.
Tenochtitlan [te-nōch'-tē-tlan'], 208.
Teton [tē'-ton], 155.
Texcoco [tec-kō'-kō], 208.
Tikal [tē'-kal], 220.
Tirawa [tē-rä'-wä], 136.
Tlacopan [tla-kō'-pan], 209.
Tlingit [tlin'-git], 189.
Tonkaway [ton'-kä-wä], 134.
Totem [tō'-tem], 98.
Tshimpshian [tcim'-cē-an], 182.
Tuscarora [tus'-kä-rō'-rä], 118.
Tutelo [tū'-tu-lō], 119.

Umane [ū-mä'-nä], 156.
Uncpapa [unk-pä'-pä], 151.
Ute [yūt], 109.
Wahpeton [wä'-pē'-ton], 155.
Wakantanka [wä'-kän-tän'-kä], 156.
Walam Olum [wä'-läm ōl'-um], 111.
Walpi [wäl'-pē], 169.
Wampampeog [wäm'-päm-pē-og], 74.
Wichita [wi'-chi-tä], 134.
Winnebago [wi'-nē-bä'-gō], 155.
Yanktonnais [yank'-ton-ā], 155.
Yetl [yātl], 189.
Zizania [zē-zā-nē-ä], 109.
Zuñi [zūn'-yē], 89.

INDEX.

Hut rings, 105.
Hypnotism, 83.

Idol, 213.
Indian, 1.
Indian Territory, 143, 223.
Initiation, 129.
Iowa, 93, 106.
IROQUOIS, 39, 53, 66, 74, 108, 115 *et seq.*, 129, 209; ball play, 29; houses, 7; story, 32; torture, 45.
Itztapalapa, 55.

Jacket, 16, 17.
Jackson, H. H., 147, 202, 225.
Jemison, Mary, 122 *et seq.*
Jemison, T., 122.
Jesuits, 206.
Journeys of George Catlin, 148.

Keeper of the belts, 75.
Kentucky, 95.
Kilts, 20, 21.
King Philip, 74, 108.
KIOWA, 60, 61.
Kisi, 170 *et seq.*
KOSKIMO, 183.
KWAKIUTL, 182.

Lacrosse, 29.
Ladders, 163.
Land in severalty, 225 *et seq.*
Languages, 2.
Lapham, I. A., 107.
Leggings, 15, 17.
Leland, C. G., 38, 83.
LENAPE, 108, 109 *et seq.*
Life: of cliff-dwellers, etc., 181; Mayan peoples, 220.
LIPAN, 56, 134.
Lip piercing, 183.
Lip plug, 183, 210.
Little Bear, 151 *et seq.*
Lone Dog, 67, 69.

Long House, 7, 119.
Lorillard City, 220.
Los Angeles, Cal., 207.
Los Cerillos, N. M., 77.
Louisiana, 135.
Lower California, 206.
Lummis, C. F., 204.

Magicians (see medicine men).
Maguey, 71, 210.
Mallery, G., 65.
Mancos Cañon, 176, 179.
MANDAN, 90, 148, 153, 155, 159; house, 11; bull-boat, 53.
Manta, 169.
Map, 3, 201, 225.
Martha's Vineyard, Mass., 51.
Mason, O. T., 30.
Massacre, 125.
Massasoit, 108.
Matthews, W., 153, 154.
Matting, 10.
MAYA, 215 *et seq.*
McElmo Cañon, 181.
Meal: acorn, 203; sacred, 90.
Measure, arrow, 50.
Medicinal liquid, 133.
Medicine, 80.
Medicine man, 33, 80 *et seq.*; performances, 83; tested, 84.
Memory helps, 66, 75.
Mendoza, 73.
Mesa, 161.
Mescal, 204.
Metate, 167, 180.
Mexico, 27, 39, 55, 71, 135, 136, 175, 206, 208 *et seq.*, 215.
Micam, 66.
Miko, 131.
Milky Way, 38.
Mission Indians, 201, 206 *et seq.*
Mission work, 227.
Missionaries, 197.
Mississippi Valley, 97.

242 INDEX.

Milton Keynes UK
Ingram Content Group UK Ltd.
UKHW021907291223
435208UK00004B/134

9 781016 460149